AIR TRANSPORTATION
PROFESSIONALS

PRACTICAL CAREER GUIDES

Series Editor: Kezia Endsley

Air Transportation Professionals, by Tracy Brown Hamilton
Childcare Professionals, by Tracy Brown Hamilton
Clean Energy Technicians, by Marcia Santore
Computer Game Development and Animation, by Tracy Brown Hamilton
Craft Artists, by Marcia Santore
Criminal Justice Professionals, by Kezia Endsley
Culinary Arts, by Tracy Brown Hamilton
Dental Assistants and Hygienists, by Kezia Endsley
Digital Communications Professionals, by Kezia Endsley
Education Professionals, by Kezia Endsley
Electricians, by Marcia Santore
Financial Managers, by Marcia Santore
Fine Artists, by Marcia Santore
First Responders, by Kezia Endsley
Ground Transportation Professionals, by Marcia Santore
Health and Fitness Professionals, by Kezia Endsley
Information Technology (IT) Professionals, by Erik Dafforn
Marketing Professionals, by Kezia Endsley
Mathematicians and Statisticians, by Kezia Endsley
Media and Journalism Professionals, by Tracy Brown Hamilton
Medical Office Professionals, by Marcia Santore
Medical Technicians, by Kezia Endsley
Multimedia and Graphic Designers, by Kezia Endsley
Nursing Professionals, by Kezia Endsley
Plumbers, by Marcia Santore
Real Estate Professionals, by Tracy Brown Hamilton
Skilled Trade Professionals, by Corbin Collins
Social Workers, by Tracy Brown Hamilton
Substance Abuse Counselors, by Tracy Brown Hamilton
Veterinarian Technicians and Assistants, by Kezia Endsley
Writers and Authors, by Tracy Brown Hamilton

AIR TRANSPORTATION PROFESSIONALS

A Practical Career Guide

TRACY BROWN HAMILTON

ROWMAN & LITTLEFIELD
Lanham • Boulder • New York • London

Published by Rowman & Littlefield
An imprint of The Rowman & Littlefield Publishing Group, Inc.
4501 Forbes Boulevard, Suite 200, Lanham, Maryland 20706
www.rowman.com

86-90 Paul Street, London EC2A 4NE, United Kingdom

British Library Cataloguing in Publication Information Available

Library of Congress Cataloging-in-Publication Data
Names: Hamilton, Tracy Brown, author.
Title: Air transportation professionals : a practical career guide / Tracy
    Brown Hamilton.
Other titles: Practical career guides.
Description: Lanham, Maryland : Rowman & Littlefield, [2022] | Series:
    Practical career guides | Includes bibliographical references and index.
    | Summary: "Air Transportation Professionals: A Practical Career Guide
    covers the steps you need to take have a career in this field, and
    includes interviews with professionals currently working in this
    field"—Provided by publisher.
Identifiers: LCCN 2022020352 (print) | LCCN 2022020353 (ebook) | ISBN
    9781538144770 (paperback) | ISBN 9781538144787 (epub)
Subjects: LCSH: Aeronautics, Commercial—Vocational guidance. |
    Aeronautics—Vocational guidance. | Career development.
Classification: LCC TL561 .H35 2022 (print) | LCC TL561 (ebook) | DDC
    629.13023—dc23/eng/20220711
LC record available at https://lccn.loc.gov/2022020352
LC ebook record available at https://lccn.loc.gov/2022020353

Contents

Introduction

Welcome to the Air Transport Industry

Welcome to the world of air transport! This book is the ideal start for understanding the various careers available to you within the air transport industry, which one is right for you, and what path you should follow to ensure you have all the training, education, and experience needed to succeed.

Air transport is an exciting and ever-evolving field. Although the first thought many have when thinking about careers related to air transport is that of pilot, there are a lot of other jobs to consider if it is your dream to join the industry. Behind every successful flight are professionals who must fulfill their duties in order for air travel to be safe, efficient, and reliable.

From air traffic controllers, who guide air transport traffic, to flight attendants, who ensure the safety and comfort of passengers, to the people who provide food and beverages on board, there are many, many paths to joining the air transport industry. Having so many paths to choose from is exciting, but it can also make it difficult to choose which is the best fit for you. This book will cover several of the options to help you narrow them down.

A Career in the Air Transport Industry

The world relies heavily on air transport, for the shipment of goods and for recreational and business travel, as well as the protection of international borders and rescue operations for natural disasters.

Air travel provides the fastest means of transport because it avoids physical obstacles such as mountain ranges and bodies of water, and it does not require that roads and railroad tracks be maintained. Although the industry suffered major losses during the COVID-19 pandemic, the world relies on the air transport industry because it is necessary, so it is a good career choice. This book will focus on the most common air transport jobs, including the following:

- Pilot and copilot
- Air traffic controller
- Aircraft and avionics mechanic
- Airport manager
- Transportation security screener
- Airfield operations specialist
- Aeronautical engineer
- Flight attendant

It will describe the functions of these jobs, as well as how they interconnect. For many, the education and experience required for a successful career vary a great deal, while for other cases there is some overlap. This will also be explained in the book.

The Market Today

How does the job market look for young people seeking to enter the field of air transport? It's been a very strange time for the industry, to say the least. The global pandemic hit the industry very hard. Travel restrictions and changes in the thinking and behavior of customers in terms of business and recreational travel caused a massive reduction in demand for air transport services, sending the industry into a spiral; many airlines had to file for bankruptcy or stop operating.

In April 2020, the International Air Transport Association issued a report stating that passenger air transport measured as revenue passenger kilometer was down 90 percent year on year in April 2020 and still down 75 percent in August. The collapse in economic activity and trade affected freight, which was almost 30 percent lower year on year in April and still about 12 percent lower in August.[1]

Although recovery has begun as we come out of the pandemic, it's unclear whether things will return to the pre-COVID-19 "normal" for the industry. According to statistics gathered by Data USA, as of November 2020, the air transport industry employed 347,000 people, which is a 16.7 percent decrease in employment when compared to November 2019.[2]

Many people think of pilots when considering working in the air transport industry—which is a very exciting job to have—but in fact pilot is only one of many career options you will find available in air transport. *humonia/iStock/Getty Images.*

It will probably come as no surprise that the best geographical location to live in if you want to work in the air transport industry is near an airport. According to Statista.com,[3] the number of public use airports in the United States has fallen since 1990, whereas the number of private use airports has increased. As of 2020, there were 5,217 public airports in the United States, which was down from 5,589 in 1990. However, the number of private airports increased over this period from 11,901 to 14,702.

Living near a so-called hub city of a commercial airline will increase your employment opportunities, through airport size alone. A "hub" refers to a city where airlines have a heavy presence due to the "hub-and-spoke" system that airlines use to route flights in a way that few aircraft are needed. This means instead of having each flight be point to point or "direct," flights from various origins ("spokes") fly via hub cities where passengers can transfer to continuing flights. The following are the top ten major airline hub cities in the United States:

- New York LaGuardia Airport (LGA)
- New York John F. Kennedy International Airport (JFK)

- Philadelphia International Airport (PHL)
- Washington Ronald Reagan National Airport (DCA)
- Charlotte Douglas International Airport (CLT)
- Miami International Airport (MIA)
- Chicago O'Hare International Airport (ORD)
- Dallas–Fort Worth International Airport (DFW)
- Phoenix Sky Harbor International Airport (PHX)
- Los Angeles International Airport (LAX)

"For me the best part of my job is meeting new people. I find people fascinating and we're so alike and different at the same time. Pre-corona [COVID-19], you'd normally connect to one or two passengers, find out their reason for flying—sometimes it's really interesting, romantic, or work related, and others it can be really sad or moving, you just never know. Especially when you fly the same route often, you start to recognize some of the frequent flyers and can greet them differently."—Carrie Blenkisop, flight attendant in Amsterdam, the Netherlands

What Does This Book Cover?

This book covers the following topics for all the aforementioned careers, as well as others:

- What kind of job best suits your personality and preference for working conditions, hours, educational requirements, work culture, and atmosphere. The book will describe the day-to-day activities involved in each job and what a typical day at work will look like.
- How to form a career plan—starting now, wherever you are in your education—and how to start taking the steps that will best lead to success
- Educational requirements and opportunities and how to fulfill them
- Writing your résumé, interviewing, networking, and applying for jobs
- Resources for further information

Once you've read the book, you will be well on your way to understanding what kind of career you want, what you can expect from it, and how to go about planning and beginning your path.

Where Do You Start?

All the jobs we cover in this book require at minimum a high school degree or equivalent, such as a General Educational Development (GED) degree, and some on-the-job training. Others require a four-year degree and even a master's degree—and of course various licensure and certification depending on the job in question.

A lot of choosing the right career for you will also depend on your personality and interests outside of work—such as whether you work better with people or independently; whether you want to be the boss or work for someone you admire; what you want your life to include outside of working hours—including hobbies and other activities that are important to you; and so on.

In the case of air transport, how you respond to and manage stress, how well you adhere to regulations and guard classified information, and how reliable you are to protect the security of others will all be major factors to your success.

Thinking about the future and your profession is exciting and also a bit daunting. With this book, you will be on track for understanding and following the steps to get yourself on the way to a happy and successful future in the air transport industry. Let's get started!

Why Choose a Career in Air Transportation?

*A*re you interested in an exciting career that offers unique benefits and exposure to various job functions, cultures, and areas of the world? Are you looking for a challenging future in an industry that the world relies on for transporting goods and people (as well as animals) globally in a way that is safe and reliable? Air transport is a niche industry that offers all these qualities and more—which we will cover in more depth in this chapter.

The fact that you are reading this book indicates that you are ready to take your curiosity; interest in technology, security, and safety; and appreciation for travel and transport to the next level: considering a career in the air transport industry. Choosing a career is a difficult task, but as we discuss in more detail in chapter 2, there are many methods and means of support to help you refine your career goal and home in on a profession that will be satisfying and will fit you the best.

Of course the first step is understanding what a particular field—in this case the air transport field—actually encompasses and informing yourself of how the future of the profession looks. That is the emphasis of this chapter, which looks at defining the field in general and then more specific terms, as well as examining the past and predicted future of the field.

The air transport industry is a large and ever-changing one that as a whole encompasses a number of different jobs. Immediately, when one thinks about jobs in the air transport industry, one might think primarily of pilots. The industry certainly does rely on talented, qualified pilots to fly the planes (as well as other aircraft), but there are other types of careers that fall under the umbrella of air transport that are equally necessary for the industry to succeed, such as engineers, security officers, air traffic controllers, and even the companies that provide food and beverages to commercial aircraft.

Beyond that, there are different areas of air transport to consider. You can work for an airport or for a specific commercial airline. You might work in the military or at a flight school. You may fly a helicopter for your local news channel, or work for an air freight shipping company like UPS or FedEx. All these initiatives require professionals to ensure that operations run smoothly and safely.

So as with any career, there are pros and cons, which we will discuss in the chapter. In balancing the good points and less attractive points of a career, you must ask yourself whether, in the end, the positives outweigh any negatives you may discover. This chapter will also help you decide whether a career in the air transport industry is actually the right choice for you. And if you decide it is, the next chapter will further offer suggestions for how to prepare your career path, including questions to ask yourself and resources to help you determine more specifically what kind of career related to air transport suits you the very best.

What Is Air Transport?

Air transport in a nutshell refers to the movement of people and cargo (goods that people need around the world) using aircraft, mainly airplanes and helicopters. Air transport is so important because it provides the fastest and most efficient means of moving goods and people great distances in a relatively short time. It has become the most common means of achieving transport, and therefore the world relies on the industry a great deal.

Keeping the industry functioning and operating requires a lot more manpower than you might imagine. There are a lot of tasks involved in getting an aircraft safely off and back onto the ground. This book will cover most of the primary jobs that fall into the "air transport" industry and are specific to it, but there are also a lot of jobs connected to air transport that are universal to other industries as well, such as administrative, financial, and legal jobs.

If you have determined for whatever reason that you are drawn to the industry as a whole—maybe you live near an airport or have family members who are pilots, for example—then you'll want to narrow down your goals by focusing on a more specific function or job. In this section, we will describe in more detail the types of air transport jobs that will be covered in the book.

PILOTS

Probably the most obvious and familiar air transport role is that of pilot. A pilot is licensed (and carefully trained) to operate aircraft, like a plane or helicopter. As part of their duties, they file flight plans, perform maintenance checks, and ensure that the craft is ready for departure. The pilot is responsible for safety items such as checking the engine, the navigation equipment, and the aircraft's systems to ensure that everything is running properly.

COPILOTS

A copilot, as the name suggests, is also a pilot, but one who flies along with the pilot. Copilots assist the pilot with the key tasks of taking off and landing the plane. A copilot will also take over for the pilot if the pilot is unable to perform their duties, for example, if they become ill midflight. Sometimes they fly aircraft for other reasons, such as charter flights, rescue operations, firefighting, aerial photography, and crop dusting.

AIR TRAFFIC CONTROLLERS

You've probably mostly seen air traffic controllers at work during scenes of tension in movies or on television. The air traffic controller has a very important responsibility in the air transport world: to track and direct the movement of aircraft on the ground and in the air, as well as on runways and taxiways. They communicate directly with pilots to give takeoff and landing instructions. All of this is with the goal of keeping the very heavily trafficked skies safe from collisions, maintaining efficiency and safety, and monitoring flights so that the status of an aircraft is always known.

AIRCRAFT AND AVIONIC MECHANICS

Aircraft and avionic mechanics are trained in keeping aircraft in safe, operating condition, in the same way that regular mechanics make sure that cars are running properly and all the parts and mechanisms of essential components like the engine are in working order. To keep an airplane in operating condition, aircraft and avionics equipment mechanics and technicians perform scheduled maintenance, make repairs, and complete inspections. The Federal Aviation Administration (FAA) sets regulations that define precise schedules that aviation mechanics must follow for checking the maintenance of various operations of aircraft.

AIRPORT MANAGERS

The airport manager has the big and potentially stressful job of ensuring that day-to-day operations of an airport are running smoothly. They are responsible for overseeing many different issues, but mainly airport safety, adherence to regulations, and budget planning.

TRANSPORTATION SECURITY SCREENERS

Transportation security screeners may seem intimidating or unfriendly at times while at work, but they have a very important responsibility that requires sharp focus. They are tasked with ensuring the safety and security of airline passengers, which entails monitoring, inspecting, and sometimes searching passengers and their bags. They check boarding passes and identification. They also identify and screen suspicious bags and confiscate prohibited items based on rules and regulations they are required to follow (if you've ever had your water bottle confiscated at the gate, you know this can be annoying—but it's also for your safety).

AIRFIELD OPERATIONS SPECIALISTS

Airfield operations specialists have another very important role in the air transport industry: they ensure the safety of takeoff and landing of commercial and military aircraft. This includes coordination between air traffic control and maintenance personnel, using airfield landing and navigational aids, implementing airfield safety procedures, monitoring and maintaining flight records, and applying knowledge of weather information.

AEROSPACE ENGINEERS

This is a very exciting career choice if you're interested in engineering and design. The aerospace engineer reviews and evaluates designs and prototypes to ensure that the products meet the standards of engineering principles. Aerospace engineers design primarily aircraft, spacecraft, satellites, and missiles—anything man-made that flies, basically.

FLIGHT ATTENDANTS

The flight attendant, also called cabin crew, may be one of the most misunderstood and undervalued jobs in the air transport industry. Their main function is not passenger service like serving beverages and ensuring other comforts, although that is part of the job when everything else is going as expected with the flight. Safety is the main function of a flight attendant. A flight attendant is there to perform safety checks before flights take off, and to demonstrate procedures like putting on oxygen masks, buckling seat belts, and using exit doors in case of emergency.

The vast number of professions and professionals that smooth and safe transport relies on may not be obvious. Air transport is a complicated process, and a field that offers exciting and demanding career opportunities for people with a wide range of skills. *baona/E +/Getty Images.*

Note: All types of skills and operational duties are required to run the air transport industry, and indeed, an airport itself runs like a mini city. For the purposes of this book, however, we will focus on careers that are most specifically related to the air transport industry.

Early First Flights

New technologies change the way we travel and transport goods as well as explore new frontiers of space and communicate with satellite technology and drones. Before it was even an industry, flight has been a fascination of humankind; its history, from its basic origins to the incredible feats we take somewhat for granted today—when any billionaire can seemingly make their way to space—is an interesting one.

Certainly the most well-known siblings of flight, Orville and Wilbur Wright flew their airplane for the first time on December 17, 1903, at Kitty Hawk in North Carolina. This celebrated first flight, captured in a famous photo, was completed by Orville at 10:35 a.m., who flew 120 feet (37 m) in twelve seconds, at a speed of only 6.8 miles per hour (10.9 km/h) over the ground. This is certainly not impressive by today's standards, but at the time this was truly a history-making accomplishment.

The fascination for flight and its realization quickly led to the development of an industry in air transport. The uses for the new technology were many, and people quickly found ways to avail of the new possibilities. Here are some of the highlights[1] of these developments:

Dawn of air freight. Proper use of flight for the delivery of goods was first demonstrated by a man named Philip Parmelee on November 7, 1920. Mr. Parmelee flew a Wright Model D airplane sixty-five miles from the city of Dayton, Ohio, to Columbus, Ohio, bringing with him two hundred pounds of silk intended for use in the opening of a department store. This first flight for freight purposes took fifty-seven minutes to complete.

Using flight for the delivery of mail. Delivering of post—goods, yes, but also good old-fashioned personal and business letters—is a key purpose of air transport, and the first known use of airplanes for the delivery of mail took place on February 18, 1911, in then-British-ruled India. British aviation pioneer Sir Walter Windham had organized an exhibition to showcase aviation, and he got permission from the postmaster general in India to operate this air mail service to promote it.

The first scheduled air mail postal service. This was another project of Sir Walter Windham and took place on September 9, 1911, between the London suburb of Hendon and the postmaster general's office in Windsor, Berkshire, UK.

Airplanes in war. The first use of an airplane in war was on October 23, 1911, during the Italo-Turkish War, when an Italian pilot made a one-hour reconnaissance flight over enemy positions near Tripoli, Libya, in a Blériot XI monoplane.

Although early attempts at basic air flight may look overly simplistic if not downright dangerous to the modern eye, these brave and groundbreaking experiments paved the way for the development of modern aircraft. *Chris Lyon/iStock/Getty Images.*

The Pros and Cons of the Air Transport Industry

As with any career, a career in air transport has upsides and downsides. Also true is that one person's "pro" is another person's "con," and the air transport industry is no exception. If you love collaborating with people, have a mind and personality for following guidelines and adhering to procedures, and aren't attached to a strictly Monday-to-Friday, nine-to-five kind of a job, the air transport industry may be for you. If you can handle stress under pressure, enjoy the challenge and excitement of not having any day at the job be just like another, that is another positive sign. But if any of these points put you off or don't fit into the way you see your career life fitting in with the rest of your life, you may need to consider that carefully.

Another consideration of a career in air transport is its stability. The air transport industry is one that we can argue is essential and therefore will always be stable, but as we have seen with the COVID-19 pandemic and as people become more conscious of carbon footprints and flying less frequently unless it's required, the ways in which we rely on the industry can shift depending on many uncontrollable, unpredictable circumstances.

Also consider that, particularly if you want to be a pilot, the field is very competitive. On the plus side, it provides a lasting challenge, continuous opportunities for learning, and a job in which travel potential is high and the chance to meet and work with interesting people from around the world is exceptional. These are all wonderful characteristics unique to a job in the air transport industry.

> **Tip:** Although it's one thing to read about the pros and cons of a particular career, the best way to really get a feel for what a typical day is like on the job and what the challenges and rewards are is to talk to someone who is already working in the profession, or who has in the past.

Although each profession within the air transport industry is different, there are some generalizations that can be made when it comes to what is most challenging about the field and what is most gratifying. Here are some general pros:

- You get to do what you love, being directly involved in the delivery of goods and people in an essential and inherently international industry.
- It is a constantly evolving field with new trends and innovations and an endless opportunity for learning.
- With technology, health, and political circumstances changing regularly, your job, its function, and its policies will shift, making the job continuously challenging, educational, and never boring.
- In this competitive field, you will have colleagues who share your passion and from whom you can learn.
- There's a vast degree of variety in work environments, depending on the type of job you want to have within the industry.
- It's a field in which you can make a real difference, getting people and goods to where they need to be for any number of purposes, safely and efficiently.

And here are some general cons:

- The working hours can be very long and irregular. You can spend days and nights on call on top of the hours you actually have to work. And because flight is involved, it's a round-the-clock industry.
- As far as salaries, they vary—a lot.
- It is a high-pressure field that requires an ability to manage stress well and multitask.
- It is an extremely competitive field, and breaking in and then advancing to the next level can take a lot of time, hard work, and patience.

"We really help pilots; we are their eyes in the sky. We know the area, the airports; we gather information regarding turbulence, clouds, and pass that information back to the pilots. When a pilot has problems with the aircraft, we can help and make sure that the airspace is free around him. We can help to get [passengers] safely but also efficiently and comfortably to their destination. That's the biggest satisfaction."— Simone Brito, air traffic controller

Is an Air Transport Career Right for Me?

This is a tough question to answer, because really the answer can only come from you. But don't despair; there are plenty of resources both online and elsewhere that can help you find the answer by guiding you through the types of questions and considerations that will bring you to your conclusion. These are covered in more detail in chapter 2. But for now, let's look at the general demands and responsibilities of an air transport career—as were mentioned previously in the section on pros and cons—and suggest some questions that may help you discover whether such a profession is a good match for your personality, interests, and the general lifestyle you want to keep in the future.

Note: Of course no job is going to match your personality exactly or fit your every desire, especially when you are just starting out. There are, however, some aspects to a job that may be so unappealing or simply mismatched that you may decide to opt for something else, or equally you may be so drawn to a feature of a job that any downsides are not that important.

Obviously having a passion for travel, international environments, and respecting and adhering to policies and guidelines, as well as a passion for continuously learning, is key to success in this field, but there are other factors to keep in mind. One way to see if you may be cut out for a career in air transport is to ask yourself the following questions:

Would I prefer to be active and moving around during work, or would I rather mostly stay put behind a desk? Depending on the type of job you pursue in the industry, you may find yourself sitting behind a desk, but you may also find yourself on your feet most of the day, or carrying heavy items or operating machinery.

When something goes wrong, can I think quickly on my feet to find a solution? Do I have the leadership skills to direct others to problem solve? Regardless of the job you have, working in the air transport industry will almost certainly require the ability to make safe, sensible, but quick decisions; direct others (including customers) to follow instructions; and deal with complaints and difficulties of passengers and other clients.

Do I have a customer service mentality and the ability to deal calmly with the public while doing my job responsibly? At the end of the day, air transport is about pleasing customers—be they waiting for a flight or waiting for an important package to be delivered. Are you able to deal with unhappy customers?

Can I consistently deal with people in a professional, friendly way? Communication—naturally—is key to success in any field, but particularly in a fast-paced, efficiency- and time-focused industry like the air transport one, your interpersonal communication will be enormously important, both with the people you work with and the people you serve.

Do I have an attention to detail and an inability to leave any stone unturned? If you work in security, or as a mechanic, or as a pilot or air traffic controller, your attention to detail is paramount in doing your job safely and well. This is also true for other roles, of course. Following guidelines and having strong observation skills are required.

AIR TRANSPORT CAREERS RUN IN THE FAMILY

Carrie Edwards. *Courtesy of Carrie Edwards.*

Carrie Edwards is thirty-nine years old and a single mom to two children, of whom she shares custody with their father. She has been a flight attendant for thirteen years, working for an airline with a hub in Amsterdam, the Netherlands. Carrie finds a lot of fulfillment in her career choice, which fits in well with her personal life. "In 2017 I had a burnout," Carrie says, "and struggled with a work/life balance. Now I own my own house in a child-friendly area, have amazing neighbors, and have no one telling me how to live my life. In my free time, you can find me in the gym or in the garden. My friends and family mean everything to me so I try and see them as much as I can too. I love my job and I love my life."

How did you choose flight attendant as a career?

Sitting around the dinner table when I was in my late teens, the conversation was often about my parents' jobs. My step-father was a pilot, my mother worked in the back office at Schiphol [Amsterdam Airport] and dealt with the pilots and passengers, my brother was a baggage handler in the UK, my oldest stepbrother was going to school to be aircraft engineer, and my youngest stepbrother was on his way to become a pilot. I was the only one who didn't have anything to do with airlines or aircraft. My step-father tried many times to convince me to become a flight attendant. When I was around twenty-five I listened and applied.

Can you describe your educational/training background and career path to date?

I got my diploma as a hairstylist, did that for a few years, and got bored. My training for flight attendant lasted around four weeks with intense training and a few flights here and there. I also work for an airline in the Netherlands, so learning Dutch fluently (I am originally from Wales) was also essential.

What is a typical day on the job for you?

Typical days don't really exist; every day or flight is different. However, before every flight leaving from home, I check any new updates we need to know about, check to see what the weather is doing at the location, see who I'm flying with and how many passengers we have. I get my shirts ironed and pack my clothes. Sometimes, depending on the destination, I travel with a suitcase and other times just a trolley and a bag. My check-in time can vary also, so sometimes I prepare the day before or on the day of.

Once getting to the airport, I check in and report to the pursers. After ten minutes, we all gather in our briefing rooms and discuss the flight, flight issues, special passengers, and how the service on board will be done.

After everything has been discussed we make our way to the gate. Once at the gate, we scan the passengers; it helps to get an idea on what kind of passengers you're going to have on board. When we're on board we do our flight safety checks and check the catering and take our places, ready for the passengers. The service part of the flight is in general the same for every flight; with the longer flights we do an extra small service. And before you know it we're on the ground again welcoming the passengers to their destination.

What's the best or most satisfying part of your job?

For me the best part of my job is meeting new people. I find people fascinating, and we're so alike and different at the same time. Pre-COVID, you'd normally connect to one or two passengers, find out their reason for flying; sometimes it's really interesting, romantic, or work related, and others, it can be really sad or moving—you just never know. Especially when you fly the same route often, you start to recognize some of the frequent flyers and can greet them differently. I've heard so many stories over the years, been asked so many funny questions I could write a book. I also love that bond you make with colleagues; it is so cool. We often get asked if we know each other long when the reality is we met an hour ago; but when you're on board, with the most of us our walls don't exist and we can tell each other nearly everything, like a free therapy session. That is truly the best thing about flying my airline, the warmth we can create for our passengers. Sometimes those friendships last and other times you never see them again. The amount of knowledge I've gained from colleagues is huge.

What's the most challenging part or stressful part of your job?

The most challenging part I think is the sleep deprivation. When you fly to the West Coast of the US or to Asia, sleeping can be challenging. Most of our flights returning home are night flights, so if you can't get any sleep or sleep poorly at the destination you really feel it during the flight. I guess for me it's something I've gotten used to. I'm lucky; some colleagues really struggle with it.

The most stressful part of my job is when things don't go to plan. Whether it's a delay or when you have that one passenger that for whatever reason is not happy, most of the time it won't have anything to do with us but is somehow our fault. People can lose it out of the blue and you have to deal with it, knowing there is always a story behind the explosion. . . . During this pandemic the amount of problems with passengers has increased greatly, and it definitely takes the fun out of the job.

What has been the most surprising or unexpected thing about your work?

I think the most unexpected part is the feeling you get when you have a great crew, knowing that for the next how many days they are your family and knowing that you have someone who has your back. Not every flight is like this but more often than not.

Surprisingly are some of the questions we get asked—it can be hilarious; you think at first it's a joke but then you realize they're dead serious. Don't get me wrong, I totally understand that not everyone knows what our job exactly is or how it works outside serving you drinks and food, but some of the questions are just unreal. I once got asked if somebody's luggage had already been taken to the next flight, while they were in the aircraft and we had just landed. The realization on his face when I asked where he thought his luggage was now at the moment was priceless.

What kinds of qualities and personal attributes do you consider advantageous to doing your job successfully?

Patience, lots and lots of patience. Flights get delayed or sometimes even canceled; this is not only frustrating for yourself but sometimes more so for the passengers. As a flight attendant, you know this can happen, especially in the winter, but passengers, in general, don't expect or understand this and can get irritable, angry, or upset; even if it's not your fault they can treat you like it is. There's no point losing it, so you have to remain calm and friendly, which can be a challenge. Flexibility is needed as your roster can change at the last minute; nothing is set in stone. Empathy toward the passengers and your fellow colleagues is a great quality to have too.

How do you combat another burnout?

No idea, really. I'm still learning. Knowing there's a problem and talking about it is so important. The colleagues I have are great at listening, and there's always one person who is going or has gone through something similar so it can be a great comfort.

Summary

This chapter covered a lot of ground as far as looking more closely at the various types of professions and jobs that exist within the overarching field of air transport. The industry provides opportunity to advance in many different roles, all essential to keep air transport running safely, effectively, and successfully.

The future and growth of the air transportation industry is in an interesting place right now, with the pandemic (we hope) largely behind us but the effect on the industry as well as in broader, world terms still being felt. But the good news is that human reliance on air transport is immense. It is nearly impossible to imagine a world in which we cannot rely on aircraft to deliver people and goods, and to contribute to success in everything from conflict to exploration. Here are some ideas to take away with you as you move on to the next chapter:

- The air transport industry is a broad one that is ever changing. Being in this industry carries a lot of responsibility, regardless of the specific job you do.

- In many air transport jobs, no day is exactly like the next. Working hours and conditions (where you work and with whom) often vary.
- Jobs in this industry require you to be a reliable person who can be trusted with classified information and security details and who can follow strict guidelines.

Given all you now know about the air transport industry, you may still be questioning whether such a career is right for you. Assuming you are now more enthusiastic than ever about pursuing a career in air transport, in the next chapter we will look more closely at how you can refine your choice to a more specific job. It offers tips and advice and how to find the role and work environment that will be most satisfying to you, and what steps you can start taking—immediately!—toward reaching your future career goals.

2

Forming a Career Plan

*C*hoosing a career may seem like one of the most difficult choices you will have to make, because it is one of the most important and there are so many options to consider. But it should not feel scary or daunting—it's actually a very exciting thing to think about. Often, it's easy to narrow down what type of careers suit your interests and personality, as we've seen in chapter 1. Other times, you can imagine yourself in many seemingly different careers, which is why it's important to think about what kinds of skills or characteristics or interests are at the root of your career ambitions.

There are simply so many types of careers out there, and it is easy to feel overwhelmed. Particularly if you have many passions and interests, it can be hard to narrow your options down. If you are looking for an exciting career that involves technology and an international environment, then the air transportation industry is definitely worth looking into, and that you are reading this book means you have decided to investigate a career in the field more closely.

But even within the air transportation field, there are many types of jobs to choose from, including what role you want to pursue, in what environment you desire to work, and what type of work schedule best fits your lifestyle.

It's a lot to think about, but fortunately it's also exciting to consider your options, particularly as it's a decision that is primarily based on aspects of you (your interests, natural gifts, curiosities) that you know more about than anyone else.

Tip: This may all sound very overwhelming. Keep in mind as you consider your career options that it is common to change your mind or shift gears at any stage in your career. Be thoughtful about your decisions, but don't put too much pressure on yourself. It's not a case of only getting one chance to decide.

Before you can plan the path to a successful career in the air transport field—such as by committing to a college program—it's helpful to develop an understanding of what role you want to have and in what environment you wish to work. Do you want to work in an established organization, or do you prefer the more entrepreneurial feel of your own business? Are you willing to relocate for your job? Work long hours and weekends? Do you want to work with people in teams, or do you prefer working more independently? These are all things to consider.

Also important to think about: How much education would you like to pursue? Depending on your ultimate career goal, the steps to getting there differ. Careers in air transport will require varying levels of qualifications, from certifications to university degrees, so the education you will need to pursue beyond receiving a high school diploma or equivalent will vary based on the job you want to have.

Deciding on a career means asking yourself big questions, but there are several tools and assessment tests that can help you determine what your personal strengths and aptitudes are and with which career fields and environments they best align. These tools guide you to think about important factors in choosing a career path, such as how you respond to pressure and how effectively—and how much you enjoy—working and communicating with people. These will be discussed in this chapter as well.

Your Passions, Abilities, and Interests: In Job Form!

Think about how you've done at school and how things have worked out at any temporary or part-time jobs you've had so far. What are you really good at, in your opinion? And what have other people told you you're good at? What are you not very good at right now, but you would like to become better at? What are you not very good at, and you're okay with not getting better at?

Now forget about work for a minute. In fact, forget about needing to ever have a job again. You won the lottery—congratulations. Now answer these questions: What are your favorite three ways of spending your time? For each one of those things, can you describe why you think you in particular are attracted to it? If you could get up tomorrow and do anything you wanted all day long, what would it be? These questions can be fun but can also lead you to your true passions. The next step is to find the job that sparks your passions.

This chapter explores the educational requirements for various careers within the air transport field, as well as options for where to go for help when planning your path to the career you want. It offers advice on how to begin preparing for your career path at any age or stage in your education, including in high school.

Planning the Plan

So where to begin? Before taking the leap and applying to or committing in your mind to a particular college or program, there are other considerations and steps you can take to map out your plan for pursuing your career. Preparing your career plan begins with developing a clear understanding of what your actual career goal is.

Planning your career path means asking yourself questions that will help shape a clearer picture of what your long-term career goals are and what steps to take to achieve them. When considering these questions, it's important to prioritize your answers—when listing your skills, for example, put them in order of strongest to weakest. When considering questions relating to how you want to balance your career with your nonwork life, such as family and hobbies, really think about what your top priorities are and in what order.

The following are questions that are helpful to think about deeply when planning your career path:

- Think about your interests outside of the work context. How do you like to spend your free time? What inspires you? What kind of people do you like to surround yourself with, and how do you best learn? What do you really love doing?
- Brainstorm a list of the various career choices within the air transportation field that you are interested in pursuing. Are you interested in organization and efficiency planning? Are you interested in helping people or maintaining security? Are you more drawn to the international aspect of air transport, working with people from if not traveling to countries around the world? Organize the list in order of which careers you find

most appealing, and then list what it is about each that attracts you. This can be anything from work environment to geographical location to the degree in which you would work with other people in a particular role.

- Research information on each job on your career choices list. You can find job descriptions, salary indications, career outlook, and educational requirements information online, for example. Some of this information was provided in chapter 1 of this book.
- Consider your personality traits. This is very important to finding which jobs "fit" you and which almost certainly do not. How do you respond to stress and pressure? Do you consider yourself a strong communicator? Do you work well in teams or prefer to work independently? Do you consider yourself a creative thinker? How do you respond to criticism? Are you curious and thorough? All of these are important to keep in mind to ensure you choose a career path that makes you happy and in which you can thrive.
- Although a career choice is obviously a huge factor in your future, it's important to consider what other factors feature in your vision of your ideal life. Think about how your career will fit in with the rest of your life, including whether you want to live in a big city or small town, how much flexibility you want in your schedule, how much autonomy you want in your work, and what your ultimate career goal is.
- Any job related to air transport or airports in particular will require certain character traits. Safety and security will always be an important factor in your job, no matter what role you find yourself in. Are you open to background checks and drug tests? Can you be trusted to keep classified information protected? Do you respect and follow protocol? These are important for any career within air transportation.
- Many job opportunities that offer experience to newcomers and recent graduates can come with relatively low salaries. What are your pay expectations, now and in the future?

Posing these questions to yourself and thinking about them deeply and answering them honestly will help make your career goals clearer and guide you in knowing which steps you will need to take to get there.

For any career path that has you working in an airport, you will be expected to follow protocol for all safety and security measures, and to be able to be trusted with classified information. *ALotOfPeople/ iStock/Getty Images.*

Where to Go for Help

Again, the process of deciding on and planning a career path can be a little bit daunting. In many ways, the range of choices of careers available today is a wonderful thing. It allows us to refine our career goals and customize them to our own lives and personalities. In other ways, though, too much choice can be extremely confusing and require a lot of soul searching to navigate clearly.

Note: Depending on your age and educational level, you might also be thinking you have time to consider these points more carefully. But the sooner you start thinking in terms of a particular career path, the better prepared you will be to spot opportunities that present themselves in your schooling or your life to advance your relative skill sets.

Career Options for Pilots You Might Not Have Considered

When most of us think about professional pilots, we logically envision an airline captain flying for a commercial carrier, or perhaps a fighter pilot in the military. But in truth, there are jobs for pilots in all kinds of industries, some of which you may not have considered before. Here are just some of the more alternative career paths to holders of valid pilot licenses:

ENTERTAINMENT INDUSTRY

A so-called Hollywood pilot is a person who flies aircraft (often helicopters) to aid in the filming of a scene for television or film. A stunt pilot is a pilot who performs tricks or acrobatics with aircraft, like you might see at an air show.

Aerial photographers and cinematographers are also employed to help create shots for film and television. News pilots work for media organizations, and tour company pilots are hired to fly visitors to an area to give an aerial tour, such as a pilot who operates flight tours of the Grand Canyon.

LAW ENFORCEMENT

Pilots are used in law enforcement to perform search and rescue of an area by air. There are police and border control pilots, as well as pilots who work for fire departments.

MEDICAL FIELD

Emergency medical pilots help people in need get to proper medical care quickly. Air ambulances can provide more advanced medical care, and air evacuation units are used to rescue people from difficult-to-access places.

AGRICULTURE

In the agriculture sector, pilots help to manage livestock, work in pest control, aid in logging, and spray crops.

UTILITIES

Pilots are used in surveying gas lines, power lines, and telephone lines.

* * *

Answering questions about your habits, preferences, interests, and personality can be very hard to do—and to do honestly. Identifying and prioritizing all your ambitions, interests, and passions is tough. It's not always easy to see ourselves objectively or see a way to achieve what matters most to us. But there are several resources and approaches to help guide you in drawing conclusions about these important questions:

- Take a career assessment test to help you answer questions about what career best suits you. There are several available online, which you can find via your search engine.
- Consult with a career or personal coach to help you refine your understanding of your goals and how to pursue them.
- Talk with professionals working in the job you are considering and ask them what they enjoy about their work, what they find the most challenging, and what path they followed to get there.
- Educate yourself as much as possible about the field: What are the latest business trends or technological advancements? Stay current as much as possible with topics relating to the career you wish to pursue.
- Although it may not be possible to "job shadow"—accompany someone during their workday to witness firsthand what a typical day on the job is like—some air transport professionals for security reasons, you may be able to get a tour of an air traffic control flight tower or the cockpit of an airplane. Your best bet may be at a small, local airport.

Online Resources to Help You Plan Your Path

The Internet is an excellent source of advice and assessment tools that can help you find and figure out how to pursue your career path. Some of these tools focus on an individual's personality and aptitude; others can help you identify and improve your skills to prepare for your career.

In addition to these sites below, you can use the Internet to find a career or life coach near you—many offer their services online as well. Job sites such as LinkedIn are a good place to search for people working in a profession you'd like to learn more about or to explore the types of jobs available in air transport.

- At educations.com, you will find a career test designed to help you find the job of your dreams. Visit https://www.educations.com/career-test to take the test.
- The Princeton Review has created a career quiz that focuses on personal interests: https://www.princetonreview.com/quiz/career-quiz.
- The Bureau of Labor Statistics provides information, including quizzes and videos, to help students up to grade twelve explore various career paths. The site also provides general information on career prospects and salaries. Visit BLS.gov to find these resources.

Note: Young adults with disabilities can face additional challenges when planning a career path. DO-IT (Disabilities, Opportunities, Internetworking, and Technology) is an organization dedicated to promoting career and education inclusion for everyone. Its website contains a wealth of information and tools to help all young people plan a career path, including self-assessment tests and career exploration questionnaires: https://www.washington.edu/doit/preparing-career-online-tutorial.

Making High School Count

Once you have narrowed down your interests and have a fairly solid idea what type of career you want to pursue, you naturally want to start putting your career path plan into motion as quickly as you can. If you are a high school student, you may feel there isn't much you can do toward achieving your career goals—other than, of course, earning good grades and graduating.

But there are actually many ways you can make your high school years count toward your career in the air transportation industry before you have earned your high school diploma. The following section will cover how you can use this period of your education and life to better prepare you for your career goal and to ensure you keep your passion alive while improving your skill set.

Even while still in high school, there are many ways you can begin working toward your career goal. Classes in another language, in math, in interpersonal communication, and in science can all help you prepare for a career in the air transportation industry. *skynesher/E +/Getty Images.*

Courses to Take in High School

Depending on your high school and what courses are offered and that you have access to, there are many subjects that will help you prepare for a career in air transport. Beyond doing your own research into different areas of air transport and different work environments and the types of clients you may serve in the future, you can take advantage of any college prep courses your school offers, particularly in areas relating to psychology or sociology, but also in subjects such as public speaking or literature to help you strengthen your communication skills.

Tip: Everybody harbors biases in the way they think about sensitive issues such as race and sexual identity. To find out whether you have biases of which you may be unaware, check out this test online, which was developed at Harvard University: https://implicit.harvard.edu/implicit/takeatest.html.

Here are some courses, college prep or standard level, that you should pursue while in high school. Some of them may seem unrelated initially, but they will all help you prepare yourself and develop key skills.

Math. Air traffic control, mechanics, flying, engineering . . . these all require math skills.

Interpersonal communication/public speaking. These courses will be an asset in any profession, but especially in the air transportation industry. So much of your job will potentially be interacting with colleagues in teams or directly with customers. You will be communicating with many other people in the job; doing so effectively will be a major factor in your success.

A second language. One of the appealing aspects for many in the air transport industry is the chance it offers to work with people from other countries or cultures. Airports are truly international environments, whether you are working on an airplane or as security on the ground.

Business and economics. You might find yourself operating your own flight school, or overseeing the operations of an airport. Classes in business and economics will help you understand how to run or work in any business, including in the air transport industry.

> **Tip:** Taking advanced placement (AP) courses while in high school (assuming you pass the AP exam at the end of the course) may enable you to earn college credit early and skip taking elementary or introductory courses in the subject (for example, psychology) when you get to college.

How Air Transport Professionals Practice Self-Care

"Self-care" refers to the various ways people can ensure that they are looking after their own needs: eating and sleeping well, for example, or taking exercise to release energy and process thoughts in a healthy, beneficial way. Doing so can help anyone—especially people in high-stress careers—maintain their own sense of well-being so they are better prepared and able to help others and avoid burnout. The following tips for how to practice self-care are provided by licensed social worker Jane E. Shersher:[1]

Focus on your breathing. Take long, slow, deep breaths as a way of maintaining your calm and relaxing your mind. Consider setting a timer to remind yourself to breathe in this way a few times a day for a minute or two at a time. It may sound a little strange to remind yourself to breathe, but doing so in this manner can lead to noticeable results.

Do a body scan. This might also sound a bit odd, but you can help your body and mind relax by paying attention to each body part one at a time from head to toe, concentrating on it and checking for points of tension to release.

Try guided imagery. Visualize yourself in a place or an environment that helps to calm you down, inspire you, or aid you in focusing for stretches of time (a few minutes, for example). There are apps you can use to listen to soothing sounds, such as nature sounds, to help you feel calm.

Practice mindfulness. Mindfulness has certainly gained in popularity over the last several years. It is the practice of focusing your awareness on the present moment, while noticing and accepting feelings, thoughts, and bodily sensations. There are several apps that offer guided mindfulness meditations that you can try.

Practice yoga, tai chi, or qigong. These are physical exercises for the body and mind, which help with mental focus, flexibility, and balance and can reduce anxiety. You can incorporate these several times a day.

Get enough sleep. Sleep is so important that it cannot be stressed enough. Your body should be getting, on average, seven to eight hours of sleep. Try to build a routine that helps you be able to fall into a sleepy state so you can have a restful night. Exercise, diet, and winding-down routines (like taking a bath, reading a book) can help.

Educational Requirements

You will have to pursue some post–high school education to become a professional in the air transportation industry. The level of post–high school degree you pursue is up to you—but keep in mind the higher a degree you earn, the better your chances are at securing employment and earning a higher salary.

Whatever type of job you want to pursue, you should expect to have to earn at minimum a two-year associate's degree as well as pass certification or license exams, or you may choose to complete a four-year bachelor's degree, which is required for many careers. In other cases a master's or even a PhD is recommended. In addition, there are certificate programs you can earn at your community college or online to continue or broaden your education throughout your career.

> "I think the most unexpected part is the feeling you get when you have a great crew, knowing that for the next how many days they are your family and knowing that you have someone who has your back. Not every flight is like this but more often than not."—Carrie Edwards, flight attendant

WHY CHOOSE AN ASSOCIATE'S DEGREE?

This degree takes comparably shorter time and coursework to complete, as related to other advanced degrees you might consider, and if you are living near a community college, that adds a layer of convenience.

A two-year degree—called an associate's degree—is sufficient to give you a knowledge base to begin your career and can form as a basis should you decide to pursue a four-year degree later. Do keep in mind, though, that jobs in air transport are quite competitive. If you are prepared to put in the financial and time commitment to earn an associate's degree and are sure of the career goal you have set for yourself, consider earning a bachelor's instead. With so much competition out there, the more of an edge you can give yourself, the better your chances will be.

WHY CHOOSE A BACHELOR'S DEGREE?

A bachelor's degree—which usually takes four years to obtain—is a requirement for some but not all careers in the air transportation industry. But in general, the higher education you pursue, the better your odds are to advance in your career, which means more opportunity and often more compensation.

The difference between an associate's and a bachelor's degree is of course the amount of time each takes to complete. To earn a bachelor's degree, a candidate must complete forty college credits, compared with twenty for an associate's. This translates to more courses completed and a deeper exploration of degree content, even though similar content is covered in both.

Note: Even when not required, continuing your education as far as possible can help advance your career, give you an edge over the competition in the field, and give you more specific knowledge relating to your work in the air transportation industry.

WHY CHOOSE A MASTER'S DEGREE?

A master's degree is an advanced degree that usually takes two years to complete. A master's will offer you a chance to become more specialized and to build on the education and knowledge you gained while earning your bachelor's. A master's can be done directly after your bachelor's, although many people choose to work for a while in between to discover what type of master's degree is most relevant to their careers and interests. Many people also earn their master's degree while working full- or part-time.

Note: In some instances, a PhD will be required, depending on your career goals. If you have the desire to teach or perform research at the university level, you will be required to hold a PhD in a relevant subject.

FULFILLING A LIFELONG DREAM

Cameron Healey. *Courtesy of Cameron Healey.*

Cameron Healey is an expat New Zealander who has called Seattle, Washington, home for more than twenty years. He's been working on a bachelor's degree majoring in aviation management over the last several years while juggling being a dad to his twin boys and husband to his wife of more than twenty years.

"My aviation journey began in New Zealand in the early 1990s where I worked in hospitality while chipping away at my private, commercial, and C-Category flight instructor ratings [certified flight instructor (CFI) equivalent]," Healey says. "Brief stints instructing and flying tourists in a Cherokee Six followed; however, steady flying opportunities in the early nineties, in New Zealand, were particularly elusive.

"Fate would have it I would soon meet my wife, a Montana native, while traveling in the United States. She has been my greatest supporter in both life and career. However, [since I had] a young family and career in publishing well established, aviation quickly morphed into more of a 'weekend warrior' mentality with the odd weekend flight taking friends and family up for a joyride around the Pacific Northwest.

"In 2015, it was time to revisit my original aspirations of becoming an airline pilot, and after two years working hard to complete my FAA certificates and then instructing out of Paine Field, Everett, Washington, to gain additional experience, I was fortunate to join Horizon Air as a first officer flying the Embraer 175 regional jet. Of course, my lifelong commitment to learning continues as I am currently training as a flight management system or FMS instructor with the training department. With a little luck and good fortune, I will hopefully continue to fly commercially until mandatory retirement at sixty-five years young. The adage that you will never work a day in your life if you do what you love has proved true. In fact, I would also wager that 'never give up on your dreams' also holds true—if you want it bad enough. *Kia Kaha!*"

* * *

How did you choose being a pilot as a career?

Aviation for me started as young as I can remember. I'm pushing fifty, and I can remember being four years old and just being fascinated by airplanes. We used to do a weekly family drive to the local airport, which was Christchurch, and we'd just walk through the terminal. I can still remember the smell of it. The feeling of the nylon carpet. It would generate so much static electricity that, back then . . . The terminal had these open, steel beams. And when you touched them, you'd get a legitimate shock. It's fascinating the things you remember. I'd see the pilots and flight attendants and the airplanes, and there was just something that wasn't necessarily tangible for me, but it just felt right. Just felt comfortable. And I had my first trial flight when I was fifteen years old. Money was a bit tight. But my mum was able to save up some money and buy me a twenty-minute trial flight. It was only twenty minutes, but even today I remember it so vividly. It stuck with me. I was sold on it from that point. I remember saying to my parents that I wanted to be a pilot when I was older. My mum was very supportive. My dad kind of felt my head was in the clouds, said it was very competitive and maybe I should focus on going to university and getting a law degree or an economics degree. He didn't necessarily see what I saw. And I get it, I'm a dad. But for me, I didn't need any encouragement.

Can you describe your educational/training background and career path to date?

When I left high school at seventeen, I made the decision to bypass university and beat the pavement. I found a job at a five-star hotel. Long story short, I stayed in hospitality for over five years working as a concierge, helping at the front desk. I lived off my tips, and I set aside my wages and put them into flying. In the early 1990s, it was very expensive to have flight lessons. I could only afford one hour a week. So it took me four years to get my private license and my commercial license. And then after four years, my dad realized this wasn't just a pipe dream for me, and he helped me pay for the flight instructor course.

In New Zealand, and it's very similar in the US, you need to have a minimum of forty flight hours to get your private license. That's going out with an instructor plus flying solo and learning maneuvers. Forty is the minimum, but most take between forty and sixty to complete their private certificate. In today's dollars, that can be anywhere from $10,000-plus. Most people take six months to a year to get the private license. To get a commercial license, you need two hundred hours. So it takes some time to get those additional 150 hours. It took me three years. At the time, it wasn't easy to get a bank loan. I had friends with better access to capital[, which] meant they could move through the system faster and do what took me four years in eighteen months. It took me a long time, blood, sweat, and tears.

What are some challenges you have faced along the way?

Early in my training, I experienced a few check ride failures. I was gutted. First time was pure bad attitude. Flying came easy to me. My instructors thought, oh you're going to do this no problem. So I didn't prepare. I didn't have that level of maturity. After finally successfully earning my certificates, I committed not to mess around, and I was able to conquer any lingering self-doubt. However, I felt that no airline would hire me. So I earned a flight instructor certificate at twenty-two, and despite experiencing some adversity, I found a way to get through it, and from then on I tried to find a job. And it was so difficult. Jobs were few and far between. I did some instruction, I flew tourists on demand, but had no consistent work. I felt disillusioned about things. So I made the decision that I needed a break and went to the US and traveled for a few months. Had a blast. It was just what I wanted and needed at the time, and I met a girl who is now my wife. I fell in love and decided to stay in the US. I thought flying was over for me. I really did. I don't know if I was burned out from working so hard for so long. I was disappointed. I fell into publishing. It turns out, I love a challenge. I have learned that self-doubt shouldn't rule what you do. I loved publishing, developing something from scratch and building it up. I had a profitable publication, but something was missing.

What finally brought you back to flying?

For years and years, I felt that something was missing in my life. There was always a sense of unfinished business for me. For nearly twenty years, flying was always in the back of my mind. I had a friend who worked for American Airlines. He said I should consider going back to flying. I laughed, thinking I was too old. But I talked to my wife. She was incredibly supportive and knows this has always been on my wish list. So we invested more money to allow me to complete my US flying certificates including multi, instrument, commercial, and flight instructor ratings. I instructed in Seattle for about eighteen months to generate enough experience to qualify for the airlines. No American airline will consider you with fewer than fifteen hundred hours. So I got that. I had multiple offers from regional airlines. The sense of, I guess, hope—it was tangible. I thought, wow, this really might happen. I interviewed with one of the US's oldest and most respected regional airlines and got an offer. I started in 2019. I was going in with the least amount of multi-engine experience. I had three months of training, and it was the most challenging thing I'd ever done. It was like drinking from a fire hose. Each simulator was two hours of briefings followed by four hours of training followed by an hour of briefing. I dug deep. Passed everything first time. After that, I had an airline transport pilot license. I've been with the company for two years and should be upgrading to captain in about six months. I worked hard and I'm proud to say I'm living my dream. I've gone from very good money to modest, but I couldn't be happier doing what I do.

What do you love about being a pilot?

I think it's the challenge. There's no question once the main wheels leave the ground there's a magical sensation of freedom. When you look down at a building that's familiar to you, it's a different world. There's no doubt some escapism, little bit of romanticism. I love traveling. I love meeting new people. I love the personal challenge that every flight, every landing is different. You can be to a place twenty times in one month, but every flight is different. There's a real skill to maneuvering a jet whether in a snowstorm or landing in gusty wind conditions. There just is. It's an awesome challenge. I learn from tough scenarios. They make me a better pilot. I'm always looking for self-improvement and that feeling of accomplishment. There's a large degree of pride and integrity to what we do.

What kinds of qualities and personal attributes do you consider advantageous to doing your job successfully?

If you want to be a commercial pilot you have to commit. My level of commitment was very long. You've got to want it. You might fail a written or practical component of your training. That's okay. It's not the end. Think about what you can learn from it. That's what airlines want to know. They want to see how you handle a knock in self-confidence. You've got to believe in yourself. Be relentless. Don't allow anyone to say you can't do it. If you want it, and you've got to want it, then you have to be prepared to be in it for the long haul.

Summary

This chapter covered a lot of ground in terms of how to break down the challenge of not only discovering whether a career in the air transport industry is right for you and in what environment, capacity, and work culture you want to work, but also how best to prepare yourself for achieving your career goal.

In this chapter, you learned about some of the specific training and educational options, requirements, and expectations that will put you, no matter what your current education level or age, at a strong advantage in a competitive field.

Use this chapter as a guideline for how to best discover what type of career will be the right fit for you and consider what steps you can already be taking to get there. Some tips to leave you with:

- Take time to carefully consider what kind of work environment you see yourself working in, and what kind of schedule, interaction with colleagues, work culture, and responsibilities you want to have.
- Pay attention to current research and issues relating to the field of air transport and in particular to the area of the field in which you want to work.
- Talk with a professional to get a feeling for what hours they keep, what challenges they face, and what the overall job entails. Find out what education or training they completed before launching their career.
- Investigate various colleges and certification options so you can better prepare yourself for the next step in your career path (more on this in chapter 3).
- Don't feel you have to wait until you graduate from high school to begin taking steps to accomplish your career goals.

- Keep work/life balance in mind. The career you choose will be one of many adult decisions you make, and ensuring that you keep all your priorities—family, location, work schedule—in mind will help you choose the right career for you, which will make you a happier person.

3

Pursuing the Educational Path

Making decisions about your educational path can be just as complex a process as choosing a career in the first place. It is a decision that not only demands understanding what kind of education or training is required for the career you want, but also what kind of school or college you want to attend and, of course, how you are going to pay for it. Everyone has different circumstances that need to be taken into consideration, be they geographical or economical. There is a lot to consider no matter what area of study you want to pursue and depending on the type of job you want to have within the field of air transportation.

Now that you've gotten an overview of the different degree options that can prepare you for your future career as an air transport professional, this chapter will dig more deeply into how to best choose the right type of study plan for you. Even if you are years away from earning your high school diploma or equivalent, it's never too soon to start weighing your options, thinking about the application process, and of course taking time to really consider what kind of educational track and environment will suit you best.

Not everyone wants to take time to go to college or pursue additional academic-based training, and for many careers it is not required, even if recommended. However, depending on what kind of career you want to pursue in the air transport arena, some level of higher education will most likely be required. Job training, at minimum, will be required no matter what field you work in, and in some cases earning a university degree will be mandatory.

So if you are interested in and prepared to follow the post–high school (or advanced) educational path, this chapter will help you navigate the process of deciding on the type of institution you would most thrive in, determining what type of degree you want to earn, and looking into costs and how to find help in meeting them.

The chapter will also give you advice on the application process, how to prepare for any entrance exams such as the SAT or ACT that you may need to take, and how to communicate your passion, ambition, and personal experience in a personal statement. When you've completed this chapter, you should have a good sense of what kind of post–high school education is right for you and how to ensure you have the best chance of being accepted at the institution of your choice.

> **Note:** At the time of writing, the United States and beyond are coming out of a pandemic that has caused some of the traditional approaches to teaching and learning to change—hopefully just temporarily. This chapter is offering advice that assumes you will be applying to and attending educational institutions in person, which will hopefully be the case. Even if, for now, you are learning or doing "campus visits" virtually, the advice offered here is still relevant, even if the way you engage with institutions, faculty members, or other students is a bit unorthodox for the time being.

Finding a Program or School That Fits Your Personality

Before we get into the details of good schools that offer degrees in subjects related to careers in the air transport industry, it's a good idea for you to take some time to consider what "type" of school will be best for you. Just as with your future work environment, understanding how you best learn, what type of atmosphere best fits your personality, and how and where you are most likely to succeed will play a major part in how happy you will be with your choice. This section will provide some thinking points to help you refine what kind of school or program is the best fit for you.

CONSIDERING A GAP YEAR

Taking a year off between high school and college, often called a gap year, is normal, perfectly acceptable, and even increasingly seen as a strong enhancement to a college application. Particularly if you want to pursue a career in an international environment such as air transport, no matter in what capacity, having exposure to the world outside of the classroom will help you gain perspective and experience that you can immediately apply to your future work. It can help you become more empathetic, less judgmental, and a more open thinker. Because the cost of college has gone up dramatically, it literally pays for you to know going in what you want to study, and a gap year—well spent—can do lots to help you answer that question. It can also give you an opportunity to explore different places and people to help you find a deeper sense of what you'd like to study when your gap year has ended.

Some great ways to spend your gap year include joining the Peace Corps or another organization that offers opportunities for work experience. A gap year can help you see things from a new perspective. Consider enrolling in a mountaineering program or other gap year–styled program, backpacking across Europe or other countries on the cheap (be safe and bring a friend), finding a volunteer organization that furthers a cause you believe in or that complements your career aspirations, joining a Road Scholar program (see www.roadscholar .org), teaching English in another country (see https://www.gooverseas.com /blog/best-countries-for-seniors-to-teach-english-abroad for more information), or working and earning money for college!

Many students will find that they get much more out of college when they have a year to mature and to experience the real world. The American Gap Year Association reports from its alumni surveys that students who take gap years show improved civic engagement, improved college graduation rates, and improved GPAs in college. Check out https://gapyearassociation.org/ for advice and resources if you're considering a potentially life-altering experience.

If nothing else, answering questions like the following ones can help you narrow your search and focus on a smaller sampling of choices. Write your answers to these questions down somewhere where you can refer to them often, such as in your notes app on your phone:

Size. Does the size of the school matter to you? Colleges and universities range from sizes of five hundred or fewer students to twenty-five thousand students. If you are considering college or university, think about what size class you would like, and what the right instructor-to-student ratio is for you.

Community location. Would you prefer to be in a rural area, a small town, a suburban area, or a large city? How important is the location of the school in the larger world to you? Is the flexibility of an online degree or certification program attractive to you, or do you prefer more on-site, hands-on instruction?

Length of study. How many months or years do you want to put into your education before you start working professionally?

Housing options. If applicable, what kind of housing would you prefer? Dorms, off-campus apartments, and private homes are all common options.

Student body. How would you like the student body to "look"? Think about coed versus all-male and all-female settings, as well as the makeup of minorities, how many students are part-time versus full-time, and the percentage of commuter students.

Academic environment. Consider which majors are offered and at which levels of degree. Research the student-to-faculty ratio. Are the classes taught often by actual professors or more often by the teaching assistants? Find out how many internships the school typically provides to students. Are independent study or study abroad programs available in your area of interest?

Financial aid availability/cost. Does the school provide ample opportunities for scholarships, grants, work-study programs, and the like? Does cost play a role in your options? (For most people, it does.)

Support services. Investigate the strength of the academic and career placement counseling services of the school.

Social activities and athletics. Does the school offer clubs that you are interested in? Which sports are offered? Are scholarships available?

Specialized programs. Does the school offer honors programs or programs for veterans or students with disabilities or special needs?

Note: Not all of these questions are going to be important to you, and that's fine. Be sure to make note of aspects that don't matter so much to you too, such as size or location. You might change your mind as you go to visit colleges, but it's important to make note of where you are to begin with.

U.S. News & World Report puts it best when it says the college that fits you best is one that will do all these things:[1]

- Offer a degree that matches your interests and needs.
- Provide a style of instruction that matches the way you like to learn.
- Provide a level of academic rigor to match your aptitude and preparation.
- Offer a community that feels like home to you.
- Value you for what you do well.

MAKE THE MOST OF CAMPUS VISITS

If it's at all practical and feasible, you should visit the campuses of all the schools you're considering. To get a real feel for any college or university, you need to walk around the campus, spend some time in the common areas where students hang out, and sit in on a few classes. You can also sign up for campus tours, which are typically given by current students. This is another good way to see the campus and ask questions of someone who knows. Be sure to visit the specific school/building that covers your possible major as well. The website and brochures won't be able to convey that intangible feeling you'll get from a visit.

In addition to the questions listed in the earlier section in this chapter titled "Finding a Program or School That Fits Your Personality," consider these questions as well. Make a list of questions that are important to you before you visit.

- What is the makeup of the current freshman class? Is the campus diverse?
- What is the meal plan like? What are the food options?
- Where do most of the students hang out between classes? (Be sure to visit this area.)
- How long does it take to walk from one end of the campus to the other?
- What types of transportation are available for students? Does campus security provide escorts to cars, dorms, and so forth at night?

To be ready for your visit and make the most of it, consider doing the following:

- Be sure to do some research. At the least, spend some time on the college website. Make sure your questions aren't addressed adequately there first.
- Make a list of questions.
- Arrange to meet with a professor in your area of interest or to visit the specific school.
- Be prepared to answer questions about yourself and why you are interested in this school.
- Dress in neat, clean, and casual clothes. Avoid wrinkled clothing or anything with stains.
- Listen and take notes.
- Don't interrupt.
- Be positive and energetic.
- Make eye contact when someone speaks directly to you.
- Ask questions.
- Thank people for their time.

Finally, be sure to send thank-you notes or emails after the visit is over. Remind the recipient when you visited the campus and thank them for their time.

The aim of this section has been to impress upon you the importance of finding the right fit for your chosen learning institution. Take some time to paint a mental picture about the kind of university or school setting that will best complement your needs. Then read on for specifics about each degree.

Note: In the academic world, accreditation matters, and it is something you should consider when choosing a school. Accreditation is basically a seal of approval that schools promote to let prospective students feel sure the institution will provide a quality education that is worth the investment and will help graduates reach their career goals. Future employers will want to see that the program you completed has such a seal of quality, so it's something to keep in mind when choosing a school.

Determining Your Education Plan

There are many options, as mentioned, when it comes to pursuing an education in the air transportation field. These include two-year community colleges, and four-year colleges, and master's programs and PhD programs.

HOW TO HAVE A GAP YEAR DURING
(OR JUST FOLLOWING) A PANDEMIC

Although an earlier section in this chapter explored options for spending a gap year that would certainly offer invaluable experience, unfortunately currently they are not all viable options due to the coronavirus—but that does not mean there aren't enriching activities and pursuits you can engage in to make a gap year just as worthwhile.

NextAdvisor offers some tips on how to make the most of a gap year,[2] even if it is not possible to participate in a structured program such as the Peace Corps. While these tips may not seem as exciting as traveling abroad, the point of a gap year is to help you refine your interests and gain additional skills before committing yourself to a college program. Here are some options to consider:

- Learn a new skill. Learn a new language. Become an expert in building an online platform if you want to grow your own private practice or reach a broader audience in the future online. Take a photography course. It's a good time to really develop yourself in new areas that may directly or indirectly affect you in your future career, in that it can help you to look at the world and people differently.
- Read. Science has shown that reading fiction makes us more empathetic,[3] which is a key skill for anyone to improve.
- Get a job to save money for college. The coronavirus has also hit many hard financially, so taking a year to earn money before heading off to school is certainly a valuable use of your time.
- Volunteer. There are virtual volunteer programs (check out Volunteer Match.org), or you can do more local volunteering, such as buying groceries for an elderly neighbor.
- Seek out remote internships. Many people are currently working at home, and there are opportunities for interns to do the same.
- Take online classes at a local community college in a related subject.

Whether you are opting for a two-year or four-year degree—and possibly later a master's or even a PhD—you will find there are many choices. It's a good idea to select roughly five to ten schools in a realistic location (for you) that offer the degree you want to earn. If you are considering online programs, include these in your list.

Tip: Consider attending a university in your resident state (where you live and pay taxes), if possible, which will save you lots of money if you attend a state school. Private institutions don't typically discount resident student tuition costs.

Be sure you research the basic GPA and SAT or ACT requirements of each school as well. Although some community colleges do not require standardized tests for the application process, others do.

Note: If you are planning to apply to a college or program that requires the ACT or SAT, advisors recommend that students take both the ACT and the SAT during their junior year of high school (spring at the latest). You can retake these tests and use your highest score, so be sure to leave time to retake early senior year if needed. You want your best scores to be available to all the schools you're applying to by January of your senior year, which will also enable them to be considered with any scholarship applications. Keep in mind these are general timelines—be sure to check the exact deadlines and calendars of the schools to which you're applying!

THE SAT IS OPTIONAL—SHOULD I TAKE IT ANYWAY?

One of the consequences of the coronavirus pandemic as it relates to education is that many universities changed aspects of their application processes. More than half of four-year colleges and universities in the United States—a staggering percentage—decided to make entrance exams like the SAT and ACT optional in 2021,[4] and this is a change that may sustain for a lot longer.

What exactly does "test optional" mean? It varies from school to school. Be sure you know what it means for any school you are considering applying to:

- Truly test optional means you decide if you want to submit your test scores. If you do, the scores will be taken into consideration along with other parts of the application. This implies that the test scores may carry less weight when compared with the other application elements but will be considered.
- "Test-flexible" schools will allow you to submit scores for the SAT or ACT, or a different test in their place (such as an SAT Subject Test or AP test).
- "Test-blind" schools will not consider any scores, even if you include them in the application.

If you feel confident that your scores will be an asset to your application, then by all means take the test and submit the score. It will not hurt your chances and can only help them. And if you take the test and are not satisfied that the results will give your application a positive edge, then you are not obligated to submit the scores. So you really can't lose by preparing for and taking the tests.

Once you have found five to ten schools in a realistic location for you that offer the degree you want, spend some time on their websites studying the requirements for admissions. Important factors weighing on your decision of what schools to apply to should include whether you meet the requirements, your chances of getting in (but aim high!), tuition costs and availability of scholarships and grants, location, and the school's reputation and licensure/graduation rates.

Note: Most colleges and universities will list the average stats for the last class accepted to the program, which will give you a sense of your chances of acceptance.

The order of these characteristics will depend on your grades and test scores, your financial resources, your work experience, and other personal factors. Taking everything into account, you should be able to narrow your list down to the institutions or schools that best match your educational or professional goals as well as your resources and other factors such as location and duration of study.

CHOOSING AN EDUCATIONAL PATH FOR YOUR SPECIFIC CAREER GOAL

Because it is such a broad field, it is not possible to present one educational path or suggest specific schools that will apply to all the careers that fall under "air transport." The training required for a pilot will obviously be different from that required of a security officer.

In general, though, when considering what education to pursue after high school, it's good to keep some ideas in mind. For one, some schools and programs have stronger reputations than others. Although you can certainly have a successful and satisfying career and experience without going to the "number one" school in your field of study, it is a good idea to shop around, to compare different schools and get a sense of what they offer and what features of each are the most important—or least important—to you.

Keep in mind that what is "great" for one person may not be as great for someone else. What might be a perfect school for you might be too difficult, too expensive, or not rigorous enough for someone else. Keep in mind the advice of the previous sections when deciding what you really need in a school.

Consider your options in terms of what you expect to or desire to achieve as an end goal, in the context not only of your career goals but what career goals you may develop as you move forward in your career. For example, you may not need a bachelor's degree to get an entry-level job in your field of choice, but down the road, as your aspirations and experience develop, you may find having one would be a strong asset if not a set requirement.

Educational Requirements for Various Air Transport Careers

As mentioned previously, you have several different paths to a career in the air transport industry, depending on the type of job you want to do. Some require licensure while others might require an advanced university degree—some may require both. In this section, we will look at the post–high school education or training requirements for the jobs in air transport that are covered in this book. Where relevant, we will point you to the best programs for associate's, bachelor's, and master's degree programs.

PILOT/COPILOT, AIR TRAFFIC CONTROLLER, AND AEROSPACE ENGINEER

To work as a pilot or copilot professionally, you will commonly be required to hold a bachelor's degree. People who pursue becoming a pilot often earn a degree in aviation. Aviation is a term for the flying or operating of an aircraft. This pertains also to working as an engineer or an air traffic controller. To pursue any of these professions in the air transport industry, you should consider a degree in aviation.

Such degrees usually take between four and six years to complete. Aviation degrees often require some flight time as well as classroom instruction, and pilot candidates holding an aviation degree—more so than other bachelor's degrees—are looked upon favorably by hiring managers.

Note: Aviation is not the only course of study, however. To pursue a career as a pilot, engineer, or air traffic controller, you can also consider degrees such as aviation technology, aeronautical science, aerospace engineering, air traffic management, or even something more general like computer science.

A bachelor's in aviation is best suited for applicants who are strong in the areas of math and science. The degree focuses on the complexity of aircraft maintenance and the fundamentals of aviation as a whole. Here are the top ten schools for programs in aviation:[5]

Purdue University, based in West Lafayette, Indiana
Ohio University, based in Athens, Ohio
Sinclair Community College, based in Dayton, Ohio
Orange Coast College, based in Costa Mesa, California
Ivy Tech Community College, based in Indianapolis, Indiana
Western Michigan University, based in Kalamazoo, Michigan
San Jacinto Community College, based in Pasadena, Texas
University of Alaska, based in Anchorage, Alaska
The Ohio State University, based in Columbus, Ohio
Bowling Green State University, based in Bowling Green, Ohio

AIRCRAFT MECHANIC

A bachelor's degree is not a requirement for a career as an aircraft mechanic—however, keep in mind that holding a degree will only ever help you in getting employed and in advancing in your career. Associate's and bachelor's degree programs are available in disciplines related to aviation technology and management.

To qualify as an aircraft mechanic, you must complete a minimum of eighteen months of training from an FAA–approved aviation maintenance technician school. Without formal training, the FAA requires thirty months of verifiable on-the-job training before taking the certification exam. If you hold a two- or four-year degree, you may be able to take the exam faster than those without a degree.

SECURITY SCREENER

To become a Transportation Security Administration (TSA) security screener, you might hold a high school diploma—although many candidates also hold a bachelor's degree or two-year degree in criminology or a related field. Other requirements that must be met: be a US citizen or national; pass a background check, drug test, medical physical, and fitness test; and speak fluent English.

AIRFIELD OPERATIONS SPECIALIST

To qualify as an airfield specialist, you must hold a related associate's degree and have verifiable on-the-job training. Earning a degree in aviation or earning a certificate in air traffic control will all be strong assets when preparing for a career as an airfield operations specialist.

FLIGHT ATTENDANT

Becoming a flight attendant is challenging. It can take three to six months to get through the application process, and it's a highly competitive process at that. Minimum requirements are a high school diploma or equivalent and the completion of a training program. This will often be dependent on the hiring and training process of the airline to which you are specifically applying. In some cases, speaking more than one language or holding certification in first aid are also strong benefits to your application.

What's It Going to Cost You?

So, the bottom line—what will your education end up costing you? First, some good news: According to *U.S. News & World Report*, the average tuition costs for colleges fell in 2020, which went against the standard trend of cost going up each year. For private colleges, costs fell by about 5 percent; for in-state colleges, the costs fell by 4 percent, and that of out-of-state (tuition for a person attending a state school but not in their resident state) has fallen by 6 percent.[6]

Note: Also according to *U.S. News & World Report*, the cost of an out-of-state school compared with an in-state school is 72 percent higher,[7] so looking for a school in the state in which you are a resident is definitely a way to cut down the costs of your education.

This trend appears to be continuing, according to an update by *U.S. News & World Report* that looks at tuition rates for the 2021–2022 school year.[8] This comes amid some calls for a tuition discount, as the COVID-19 pandemic has forced so many institutions to move to online course delivery.

In addition, there are several financial aid options to help you find the funding to earn the degree you want. We cover those next.

School can be an expensive investment, but there are many ways to seek help paying for your education. *Hispanolistic/E +/Getty Images.*

WRITING A GREAT PERSONAL STATEMENT FOR ADMISSION

The personal statement you include with your application to college is extremely important, especially when your GPA and SAT/ACT scores are on the border of what is typically accepted. Write something that is thoughtful and conveys your understanding of the profession you are interested in, as well as your desire to practice in this field. Why are you uniquely qualified? Why are you a good fit for this university? These essays should be highly personal (the "personal" in personal statement). Will the admissions professionals who read it, along with hundreds of others, come away with a snapshot of who you really are and what you are passionate about?

Look online for some examples of good ones, which will give you a feel for what works. Be sure to check your specific school for length guidelines, format requirements, and any other guidelines they expect you to follow.

And of course, be sure to proofread it several times and ask a professional (such as your school writing center or your local library services) to proofread it as well.

Financial Aid: Finding Money for Education

Finding the money to attend college can seem out of reach. But you can do it if you have a plan before you actually start applying to college. If you get into your top-choice university, don't let the sticker cost turn you away. Financial aid can come from many different sources, and it's available to cover all different kinds of costs you'll encounter during your years in college, including tuition, fees, books, housing, and food.

The good news is that universities more often offer incentive or tuition discount aid to encourage students to attend. The market is often more competitive in the favor of the student, and colleges and universities are responding by offering more generous aid packages to a wider range of students than they used to. Here are some basic tips and pointers about the financial aid process:

- You apply for financial aid during your senior year. You must fill out the FAFSA (Free Application for Federal Student Aid) form at studentaid. gov, which can be filed starting October 1 of your senior year until June of the year you graduate. Because the amount of available aid is limited, it's best to apply as soon as you possibly can.
- Be sure to compare and contrast deals you get at different schools. There is room to negotiate with universities. The first offer for aid may not be the best you'll get.

- Wait until you receive all offers from your top schools and then use this information to negotiate with your top choice to see if it will match or beat the best aid package you received.
- To be eligible to keep and maintain your financial aid package, you must meet certain grade/GPA requirements. Be sure you are very clear on these academic expectations and keep up with them.
- You must reapply for federal aid every year.

Note: Watch out for scholarship scams! You should never be asked to pay to submit the FAFSA form ("free" is in its name) or be required to pay a lot to find appropriate aid and scholarships. These are free services. If an organization promises you you'll get aid or that you have to "act now or miss out," these are both warning signs of a less reputable organization. Also, be careful with your personal information to avoid identity theft as well. Simple things like closing and exiting your browser after visiting sites where you entered personal information goes a long way. Don't share your student aid ID number with anyone either.

It's important to understand the different forms of financial aid that are available to you. That way, you'll know how to apply for different kinds and get the best financial aid package that fits your needs and strengths. The two main categories that financial aid falls under are gift aid, which doesn't have to be repaid, and self-help aid, which can be either loans that must be repaid or work-study funds that are earned. The next sections cover the various types of financial aid that fit in one of these areas.

GRANTS

Grants typically are awarded to students who have financial needs, but they can also be awarded in the areas of athletics, academics, demographics, veteran support, and special talents. They do not have to be paid back. Grants can come from federal agencies, state agencies, specific universities, and private organizations. Most federal and state grants are based on financial need.

Examples of grants are the Pell Grant, SMART Grant, and the Federal Supplemental Educational Opportunity Grant (FSEOG). Visit the US Department of Education's Federal Student Aid site for current information about grants (see https://studentaid.ed.gov/types/grants-scholarships).

SCHOLARSHIPS

Scholarships are merit-based aid that does not have to be paid back. They are typically awarded based on academic excellence or some other special talent, such as music or art. Scholarships also fall under the areas of athletic based, minority based, aid for women, and so forth. These are typically not awarded by federal or state governments but instead come from the specific university you applied to as well as private and nonprofit organizations.

Be sure to reach out directly to the financial aid officers of the schools you want to attend. These people are great contacts who can lead you to many more sources of scholarships and financial aid. Visit http://www.gocollege.com /financial-aid/scholarships/types/ for more information about how scholarships in general work.

LOANS

Many types of loans are available especially to students to pay for their post-secondary education. However, the important thing to remember here is that loans must be paid back, with interest. Be sure you understand the interest rate you will be charged. This is the extra cost of borrowing the money and is usually a percentage of the amount you borrow. Is this fixed or will it change over time? Is the loan and interest deferred until you graduate (meaning you don't have to begin paying it off until after you graduate)? Is the loan subsidized (meaning the federal government pays the interest until you graduate)? These are all points you need to be clear about before you sign on the dotted line.

> "If you want to be a commercial pilot you have to commit. My level of commitment was very long. You've got to want it. You might fail a written or practical component of your training. That's okay. It's not the end. Think about what you can learn from it. That's what airlines want to know. They want to see how you handle a knock in self-confidence. You've got to believe in yourself. Be relentless."—Cameron Healey, pilot

There are many types of loans offered to students, including need-based loans, non-need-based loans, state loans, and private loans. Two very reputable federal loans are the Perkins Loan and the Direct Stafford Loan. For more information about student loans, start at https://bigfuture.collegeboard.org/pay-for-college/loans/types-of-college-loans.

FEDERAL WORK-STUDY

The US Federal Work-Study Program provides part-time jobs for undergraduate and graduate students with financial need so they can earn money to pay for educational expenses. The focus of such work is on community service work and work related to a student's course of study. Not all colleges and universities participate in this program, so be sure to check with the school financial aid office if this is something you are counting on. The sooner you apply, the more likely you will get the job you desire and be able to benefit from the program, as funds are limited. See https://studentaid.ed.gov/sa/types/work-study for more information about this opportunity.

A PILOT FROM BEFORE HE WAS BORN

G. Leigh Foti II. *Courtesy of G. Leigh.*

G. Leigh Foti II has held his FAA commercial helicopter rating (license to fly recreationally or for personal purposes) since the mid-1980s. He has flown all types of helicopters in high altitudes as well as at sea level in all weather conditions day and night in North America, Central America, South America, and the Caribbean and has been contracted on a freelance basis to perform various helicopter missions. In addition, Leigh Foti II has performed flight operations for aerial photography; traffic reporting; tours; sling-load operations; specialized utility missions;

natural resource missions; power, pipeline, and security patrols; and government contracts (foreign and domestic).

Leigh Foti II attended Western Carolina University in North Carolina. After completion of his aero-medical residency program at Baptist Hospital in Knoxville, Tennessee, he completed a four-year program at Western Carolina in emergency medical care with a concentration in applied kinesiology. He has also worked as a performance fitness coach since 1984 specializing in post-rehab/advanced post-rehab and corrective exercise. He is also a former resident flight paramedic.

In addition, Leigh Foti II is a former road and track cycling Category 2 and Masters cyclist, competing in six US National Masters Championship events in road and track cycling. In 2007, he competed at the World Masters Track Cycling Championship in Sydney, Australia, placing eighteenth in the world in the 3 km pursuit and eighteenth in the world in the scratch race. He has trained, coached, and rehabbed all types of clients from the Olympic athlete to the grandparent. He was a contributor to CNN and CNN World Europe's *Health Minute*, which ran in the early to mid-2000s, and, until COVID-19, was a regular presenter at the Annual Live Well Conference in New York City.

* * *

How did you choose piloting helicopters as a career?

I have wanted to fly helicopters for as long as I can remember. My eighty-eight-year-old mom told me when she was pregnant with me, she took a ride in a Bell 47 helicopter. She stated that during and just after the flight I never kicked so much in her belly in all her pregnancy. My mom said the career chose me. I started taking lessons to fly when I was a teenager. My father insisted I get my college degree. I was already paying for flight lessons; I continued flight school while starting college.

Can you describe your educational background and career path to date?

I have a BS in emergency medical care, a minor in kinesiology, and a commercial helicopter rating. I obtained my commercial helicopter rating while I was working on my college degree. I was able to work flying jobs around college classes and summer breaks. After college I worked as a paramedic and later as a flight paramedic. I worked twenty-four- and twelve-hour shifts as a medic. I worked any available helicopter jobs on my off days. When I couldn't get any flying work, I put my background in kinesiology to work as a human performance coach and post-rehab specialist. After four years of being a medic, I gave it up to focus on flying full-time. I took a full-time helicopter job while still doing coaching when I couldn't fly. I worked as a line pilot for the next ten years in the western United States. In the late nineties

I moved back to the southern US where I grew up and went to college. I haven't flown full-time in years, but I fly enough to stay current. I have been working for over twenty years with my coaching business.

What is a typical day on the job for you?

Ever changing . . . I have worn many hats in the last thirty-eight years. I was never a nine-to-five person, and every job I have ever had was always changing. I have been a contractor more than an employee. I like having more control, but it has cost me in other ways in promotions and some opportunities.

What's the best or most satisfying part of your job?

Out of my three careers, flying helicopters was most satisfying. It is a very rewarding job no matter what the mission.

What's the most challenging part or stressful part of your job?

Flying is always challenging and stressful. You must be at the top of your game. There are so many things that can go wrong in a split second.

What has been the most surprising thing about your job?

To get the best jobs many times, you give up a lot and it can take a long time to get there. Sometimes the highest-paying jobs are in the middle of nowhere.

What kinds of qualities and personal attributes do you consider advantageous to doing your job successfully?

Patience is important in aviation. Situational awareness is very important. Having the ability to listen carefully and question skillfully.

How do you combat burnout?

Because I had two and sometimes three careers going at the same time, burnout from one job didn't occur. When I felt like I was working too much, I cut back on one or two jobs.

How do you see your career or the air transport field evolving in the future?

Automated flight being electric, or hydrogen fuel cell looks promising.

━━━━━━━━━

Summary

This chapter covered aspects of college and postsecondary schooling that you'll want to consider as you move forward. Remember that finding the right fit is especially important, as it increases the chances that you'll stay in school and earn your degree as well as have an amazing experience while you're at it.

In this chapter, we discussed how to evaluate and compare your options to get the best education for the best deal. You also learned a little about scholarships and financial aid, how the SAT and ACT work, if applicable, and how to write a unique personal statement that eloquently expresses your passions.

Use this chapter as a jumping-off point to dig deeper into your particular area of interest. Some tidbits of wisdom to leave you with:

- Take the SAT and ACT early in your junior year so you have time to take them again. Most universities automatically accept the highest scores, while some schools do not require these test scores at all.
- Make sure that the institution you plan to attend has an accredited program in your field of study. And be sure you understand any licensure requirements and how they may change state to state, for example.
- Don't underestimate how important campus visits are, especially in the pursuit of finding the right academic fit. Come prepared to ask questions not addressed on the school website or in the literature.
- Your personal statement is a very important piece of your application that can set you apart from others. Take the time and energy needed to make it unique and compelling.
- Don't assume you can't afford a school based on the "sticker price." Many schools offer great scholarships and aid to qualified students. It doesn't hurt to apply. This advice especially applies to minorities, veterans, and students with disabilities.
- Don't lose sight of the fact that it's important to pursue a career that you enjoy, are good at, and are passionate about! You'll be a happier person if you do so.

At this point, your career goals and aspirations should be gelling. At the least, you should have a plan for finding out more information. Remember to do the research about the university, school, or degree program before you reach out and especially before you visit. Faculty and staff find students who ask challenging questions much more impressive than those who ask questions that can be answered by spending ten minutes on the school website.

In chapter 4, we go into detail about the next steps—writing a résumé and cover letter, interviewing well, follow-up communications, and more. This is information you can use to secure internships, volunteer positions, summer jobs, and more. It's not just for college grads. In fact, the sooner you can hone these communication skills, the better off you'll be in the professional world.

Writing Your Résumé and Interviewing

*W*ith each chapter of this book, we have narrowed the process of planning your air transport industry career path, from the broadest of strokes— what jobs exist within the field and what people who have those jobs actually do—to how to plan your strategy and educational approach to making your dream job a reality.

In this chapter we will cover the steps involved in applying for jobs or schools: how to prepare an effective, engaging, and informative résumé and slam-dunk an interview.

> **Note:** Whatever job, school, or organization you are seeking to attend or be employed in or by, how you present yourself in person and in writing will be a major determinant in your success and should receive just as much attention as the credentials you earn and the skills you hone.

Your résumé is your opportunity to summarize your experience, training, education, and goals and attract employers or school administrators. You can think of it like this: the goal of the résumé is to land the interview, and the goal of the interview is to land the job. Even if you do not have much working experience, you can still put together a résumé that expresses your interests and goals and the activities that illustrate your competence and interest.

As well as a résumé, you will be expected to write a cover letter that is basically your opportunity to reveal a little bit more about your passions, your motivation for a particular job or educational opportunity, and often to express more about you personally to give a potential employer a sense of who you are and what drives you. Let relevant personal characteristics come through where appropriate in this letter. You are applying for a job within a field where trustworthiness and attention to detail are paramount, as are communication skills, so you may not want to come across as a daredevil, for example.

Giving the right impression is undoubtedly important, but don't let that make you nervous. In a résumé, cover letter, or interview, you want to put forward your best but also your genuine self. Dress professionally, proofread carefully (spelling, grammar, and typographical errors will be noticed and will work against you!), but ensure you are being yourself.

In this chapter, we will cover all these important aspects of the job-hunting process, and by the end you will feel confident and ready to present yourself as a candidate for the job you really want.

Writing Your Résumé

Writing your first résumé can feel challenging because you have likely not yet gained a lot of experience in a professional setting. But don't fret; employers understand that you are new to the workforce or to the particular career you are seeking.

Note: The right approach is never to exaggerate or invent experience or accomplishments, but to present yourself as someone with a good work ethic and a genuine interest in the particular job or organization and to use what you can to present yourself authentically and honestly.

There are some standard elements to an effective résumé that you should be sure to include. At the top should be your name, of course, as well as email address or other contact information.

There is freedom and flexibility in how you organize the content of your résumé. The important thing is to present the most important and relevant information at the top. Your résumé needs to be easy to navigate and read. Always list your experience in chronological order, beginning with your current or most recent position—or whatever experience you want to share.

If you are a recent graduate with little work experience, you might want to begin with your education. If you've been in the working world for a while, you can opt to list your education or any certifications you have at the end.

Note: You may need to customize your résumé for different purposes to ensure you are not filling it with information that does not directly link to your qualifications for a particular job.

If this is your first résumé, be sure you highlight your education where you can—any courses you've taken, be it in high school or through a community college or any other place that offers training related to your job target. Also highlight any hobbies or volunteer experience you have. But be concise; one page is usually appropriate, especially for your very first résumé.

Tip: Before preparing your résumé, try to connect with a hiring professional—a human resources person or hiring manager—in a similar position or organization you are interested in. They can give you advice on what employers look for and what information to highlight on your résumé, as well as what types of interview questions you can expect.

As important as your résumé's content is the way you design and format it. You can find several samples online of résumés that you can be inspired by. At TheBalanceCareers.com, for example, you can find many templates and design ideas.[1] You want your résumé to be attractive to the eye and formatted in a way that makes the key points easy to spot and digest; according to some research, employers take an average of six seconds to review a résumé, so you don't have a lot of time to get across your experience and value.

SKILLS TO INCLUDE IN A PILOT'S RÉSUMÉ

For the most part, writing a résumé as a pilot or to get work as a pilot is not wildly different from writing any other kind of résumé. You want to include relevant information that highlights your qualifications for the job, including your experience as a pilot, of course, and your education and training.

But there are some specific points you will want to include, such as flight times and flight log recordings. And here are some important skills to highlight on a pilot résumé, recommended by Indeed.com:

- **Teamwork:** Pilots need strong teamwork skills to collaborate with relevant flight or airline personnel. Successful teamwork allows for a safer flight and easier communication for everyone involved in a flight.
- **Communication:** Communication skills allow you to effectively interact with airline personnel, cabin crew, air traffic control, and various officers. Communicating with air traffic control, for example, ensures you receive flight advisement on things such as weather conditions while in the air.
- **Adaptability:** Pilots use their adaptability to fly aircraft no matter the circumstances that arise while in flight. Whether you're faced with unusual weather or you're not able to land at the original destination, it's important to know what to do in [these] situations in order to get your passengers to safety.
- **Knowledge of aircraft technology and equipment:** Pilots need to know how to operate aircraft safely. In order to do this, you need to know how various aircraft components work, such as the electrics and the aircraft's engines.[2]

WRITING AN OBJECTIVE

The objective section of your résumé is one of the most important, as it is the first section a recruiter or hiring manager will read and therefore the first sense they will develop of you as a candidate. The objective should be brief but to the point. It should be focused and give a sense of you as a unique applicant—you don't want it to be generic or bland—so show how creative you can be while keeping it professional. It's important to take your time and really refine your objective so you can stand out and attract employers or clients. Here are some sample objectives for an airport professional résumé recommended by LiveCareer.com:

- Seeking a Flight Attendant position with Republic Airline, to apply 4 years of solid flight attendant experience. Coming with service orientation, polished and professional interpersonal skills, ability to process information quickly, and stress management abilities to provide safe and comfortable flight experience.

- Experienced Ramp Agent with manual dexterity and High School Diploma. Seeking to apply training and work experience as a ramp agent with Southwest Airlines, coming with sound communication skills both orally and via the radio.
- Individual with strong initiative and excellent customer relations skills. To obtain the position of Airport Front Desk Clerk with Portland International Airport where 2 years of customer service experience will be utilized. Also, bringing strong ability to handle cash and credit card transactions in an efficient and accurate manner, and great communications skills.
- Self-motivated individual with strong organizational skills and ability to perform assigned duties effectively in a fast-paced environment. Seeking the role of Airport Staff Assistant at XYZ Inc. to apply strong clerical experience. Also coming with superior clerical skills, a detail orientation, and advanced IT expertise with Microsoft Office applications.
- Energetic individual with great communication skills and High School Diploma. Desirous of an Airport Passenger Service Agent position, to apply technical and exceptional customer service skills. Bringing strong computer skills and 2 years' work experience in the aviation industry.
- Reliable and highly organized individual with strong communications skills. Seeking the position of Cabin Service Agent with Prospect Airport Services where 2 years of aviation experience and ability to perform security searches at the airport will be applied.
- Experienced aviation professional with excellent written and oral communication skills and Bachelor's degree. Desiring the position of Duty Manager with Prospect Terminal services; coming with 6+ years of aviation experience and advanced computer skills.
- Natural leader with exceptional supervisory and organizational abilities and Bachelor's degree. Interested in a General Manager, Airport Customer Experience with American Airlines. Bringing strong business acumen, advanced computer skills, and 6 years of airline operations experience to ensuring safe, reliable, and efficient service delivery.
- Technically inclined team player with great communications skills and ability to work in a time-sensitive environment. Seeking the Provisioning Agent position at Southwest Airlines; offering physical dexterity, technical skills, and strong ability to handle emergency situations.

- Energetic individual with positive attitude, teamwork abilities, and willingness to work a flexible schedule. Seeking for an Airport Operations Agent position with Prospects Airport Services, to work at DFW International Airport.[3]

Be sure you do your research about the job and the organization to which you are applying. Then you can better craft your objective to highlight the ways in which you uniquely match their needs.

WRITING YOUR COVER LETTER

As well as your résumé, most employers will ask that you submit a cover letter. This is a one-page letter in which you express your motivation, why you are interested in the organization or position, and what skills you possess that make you the right fit. Here are some tips for writing an effective cover letter:

- As always, proofread your text carefully before submitting it.
- Be sure you have a letter that is focused on a specific job. Do not make it too general or one size fits all. Your personality and uniqueness should come through, or the recruiter or hiring manager will move on to the next application.
- Summarize why you are right for the position. Keep it relevant and specific to what the particular organization is looking for in a candidate and employee.
- Keep your letter to one page whenever possible.
- Introduce yourself in a way that makes the reader want to know more about you and encourages them to review your résumé.
- Be specific about the job you are applying for. Mention the title and be sure it is correct.
- Try to find the name of the person who will receive your letter rather than keeping it nonspecific ("to whom it may concern").
- Be sure you include your contact details.
- End with a "call to action"—a request for an interview, for example.

Linking In with Impact

As well as your paper or electronic résumé, creating a LinkedIn profile is a good way to highlight your experience and promote yourself, as well as to network. Joining professional organizations and connecting with other people in your desired field are good ways to keep abreast of changes, trends, and work opportunities.

The key elements of a LinkedIn profile are your photo, your headline, and your profile summary. These are the most revealing parts of the profile and the ones employers and connections will base their impression of you on.

The photo should be carefully chosen. Remember that LinkedIn is not Facebook or Instagram; it is not the place to share a photo of you acting too casually on vacation or at a party. According to Joshua Waldman, author of *Job Searching with Social Media for Dummies*, the choice of photo should be taken seriously and be done right.[4] His tips:

- Choose a photo in which you have a nice smile.
- Dress in professional clothing.
- Ensure that the background of the photo is pleasing to the eye. According to Waldman, some colors—like green and blue—convey a feeling of trust and stability.
- Remember, it's not a mug shot. You can be creative with the angle of your photo rather than stare directly into the camera.
- Use your photo to convey some aspect of your personality.
- Focus on your face. Visitors to your profile will see only a small thumbnail image, so be sure your face takes up most of it.

Interviewing Skills

With your sparkling résumé and LinkedIn profile, you are bound to be called for an interview. This is an important stage to reach: you will have already gone through several filters—a potential employer has gotten a quick scan of your experience and has reviewed your LinkedIn profile and has made the decision to learn more about you in person.

There's no way to know ahead of time exactly what to expect in an interview, but there are many ways to prepare yourself. You can start by learning more about the person who will be interviewing you. In the same way recruiters and employers can learn about you online, you can do the same (for a business or a professional in a business). You can see if you have any education or work experience in common, or any contacts you both know. You can find out a bit about the company culture. It's perfectly acceptable and even considered proactive in a positive way to research the person with whom you'll be interviewing, such as on LinkedIn.

A job interview can be stressful. You can help calm your nerves and feel more confident if you prepare ahead by thinking about answers to questions you can anticipate being asked. *Jakob Helbig/Image Source/Getty Images.*

Preparing yourself for the types of questions you will be asked to ensure that you offer a thoughtful and meaningful response is vital to interview success. Particularly when you are applying for a job that will require you to present yourself conversationally, it is paramount that you respond in an effective, composed manner. Consider your answers carefully, and be prepared to support them with examples and anecdotes.

Here are some questions you should be prepared to be asked. It's a good idea to consider your answers carefully, without memorizing what you mean to say (as that can throw you off and will be obvious to the interviewer).

- Why did you decide to enter this field? What drives your passion for working in the air transport industry?
- What is your educational background? What credentials have you earned?
- What experience do you have relating to this job?
- Are you a team player? Describe your usual role in a team-centered work environment. Do you easily assume a leadership role?

INSPIRED BY WATCHING MY DAD FLY

Michael Harston is a former US Air Force pilot who now flies for FedEx.

* * *

How did you decide to become a pilot?

My love for aviation started as a kid, growing up on US Air Force bases and watching my dad fly. This led me to a career in the military, where I began my journey to becoming a pilot.

Can you describe your educational and career path to date?

After graduating from high school, I enlisted in the military and served as an in-flight refueling technician (boom operator) on the KC-135 for the US Air Force Reserves. After serving in this capacity for ten years, completing my bachelor's degree, and obtaining my private pilot's license, I applied to the undergraduate pilot training (UPT) program with the Seventy-Eighth Air Refueling Squadron. This entailed an Air Force Officer Qualification Test (AFOQT), interview, and board review process for pilot training selection. Upon acceptance, I attended UPT at Vance Air Force Base in Oklahoma, with specialty training for air refueling in the KC-10 aircraft. After a twenty-six-year career in the Air Force, I continued my aviation career as a first officer—flying Boeing 757, 767, and 777s for FedEx.

Michael Harston is a former US Air Force pilot who now flies for Federal Express. *jgareri/E +/Getty Images.*

What is a typical day on the job for you?

There isn't exactly a typical day. Once a month we bid to fly specific routes; these bids are awarded based on seniority. For example, two weeks ago, I bid an Asia trip, which required a sixteen-hour commute on a commercial flight, in order to pilot FedEx aircraft throughout Asia for a week (Singapore, China, Thailand, and Korea). Upon arriving in Singapore, a local liaison received us, took us through customs and immigrations, and deposited us at a hotel provided by FedEx. When time came to operate our scheduled line, FedEx provided ground transportation to the aircraft, where we began our preflight duties.

Preflight consists of (1) aircraft walk around and visual inspection, (2) flight deck inspection, (3) verification of aircraft fuel and review of weight and balance calculations, (4) computation of performance takeoff data, (5) verbal briefing of taxi and departure procedures, and (6) verbal briefing of aircraft emergency return procedures. Approximately fifteen minutes prior to takeoff, we coordinate with ground crew and airfield control to be pushed away from our gate. We then start the engine, taxi, and take off. The first officer and captain alternate flying the aircraft for each leg of the trip.

The in-flight portion: We fly a specific route, similar to a three-dimensional road map in the sky that FedEx has filed with appropriate agencies, in advance. We do not deviate from the route, unless dictated otherwise by air traffic control. Crew in-flight duties consist of aircraft control manipulation, radio communications, monitoring weather radar, terrain avoidance, and route and altitude adherence. Prior to destination arrival, the aircrew calculates landing data (approach and landing speeds) based on airfield weather and runway conditions. One pilot briefs the other on procedures for arrival, approach, and ground taxi.

Postflight: once the aircraft has reached its parking location, aircrew completes postflight inspections and either logs a new flight plan for an additional leg of the trip or deplanes for home/hotel.

What is the most satisfying part of your job?

The best part of my job is the ability to live in so many different places, worldwide. For instance, FedEx has hubs in Alaska, Tennessee, Indiana, California, Hong Kong, and Germany. This means I have the ability to live and work throughout the United States or overseas.

What is the most challenging or stressful part of your job?

(1) Recurring proficiency evaluation (aircraft and operational knowledge). Unlike many other jobs, every nine months we are assessed based on technical, practical, and operational knowledge of aviation rules and our specific aircraft. An evaluator reviews our response to multiple simulated emergencies such as engine failures on takeoff. (2) Recurring health and fitness evaluation: every six months, I am subjected to an FAA Class 1 medical analysis, the outcome of which determines whether or not I am fit to fly (allowed to work). (3) Exhaustion: FedEx is an overnight cargo carrier, which means I am often operating aircraft while sleep deprived.

What has been the most surprising thing about your job?

I think the most surprising thing to most people is probably how little human manipulation of the flight controls actually occurs on most commercial flights. Although piloting skills are necessary, especially in the event of an emergency, humans serve more as a redundancy to the autopilot during flight. Pilots typically only hand fly the aircraft for the first and last couple minutes of each flight. The most important duty of pilots in modern-day aircraft is computer flight management (in both the horizontal and vertical planes).

What qualities do you consider important to doing your job successfully?

The abilities to work with others, have technical proficiency, remain calm under pressure, adapt to new information, and have humility.

How do you combat burnout?

I combat burnout by changing scenery (flying different locations), taking time off between trips, exercising, spending time with loved ones, playing with my dog, and participating in my hobbies (hang gliding, paragliding, skiing, motorcycle riding, etc.).

How do you see your field evolving in the future?

In my opinion, aircraft will be operated by a single in-flight pilot with a remote ground-based copilot who will monitor multiple aircraft simultaneously, in case of emergency. Eventually, aircraft will fly completely autonomously with minimal human ground crew. This transition will probably begin with cargo aviation.

BEWARE WHAT YOU SHARE ON SOCIAL MEDIA

Most of us engage in social media. Sites such as Facebook, Twitter, and Instagram provide us a platform for sharing photos and memories, opinions, and life events, and reveal everything from our political stance to our sense of humor. It's a great way to connect with people around the world, but once you post something, it's accessible to anyone—including potential employers—unless you take mindful precaution.

Your posts may be public, which means you may be making the wrong impression without realizing it. More and more, people are using search engines like Google to get a sense of potential employers, colleagues, or employees, and the impression you make online can have a strong impact on how you are perceived. Approximately 70 percent of employers search for information on candidates on social media sites.[5]

Glassdoor.com offers the following tips for how to keep your social media activity from sabotaging your career success:[6]

Check your privacy settings. Ensure that your photos and posts are only accessible to the friends or contacts you want to see them. You want to come across as professional and reliable.

Rather than avoid social media while searching for a job, use it to your advantage. It's to your advantage to have an online presence (as long as it's a flattering one). Give future employers a sense of your professional interest by "liking" pages or joining groups of professional organizations related to your career goals.

Grammar counts. Be attentive to the quality of writing of all your posts and comments.

Be consistent. With each social media outlet, there is a different focus and tone of what you are communicating. LinkedIn is very professional while Facebook is far more social and relaxed. It's okay to take a different tone on various social media sites, but be sure you aren't blatantly contradicting yourself.

Choose your username carefully. Remember, social media may be the first impression anyone has of you in the professional realm.

DRESSING APPROPRIATELY

How you dress for a job interview is very important to the impression you want to make. Remember that the interview, no matter what the actual environment in which you'd be working, is your chance to present your most professional self. Although you will not likely ever wear a suit to work, for the interview it's the most professional choice.

> **Tip:** A suit is no longer an absolute requirement in many job interviews, but avoid looking too casual as it will give the impression you are not that interested.

WHAT EMPLOYERS EXPECT

Hiring managers and human resources professionals will also have certain expectations of you at an interview. The main thing is preparation: it cannot be overstated that you should arrive to an interview appropriately dressed, on time, unhurried, and ready to answer—and ask—questions. For any job interview, these are the main things you should do:

- Have a thorough understanding of the organization and the job for which you are applying.
- Be prepared to answer questions about yourself and your relevant experience.

- Be poised and likeable, but still professional. Employers will be looking for a sense of what it would be like to work with you on a daily basis and how your presence would fit in the culture of the business.
- Stay engaged. Listen carefully to what is being asked and offer thoughtful but concise answers. Don't blurt out answers you've memorized, but really focus on what is being asked.
- Be prepared to ask your own questions. It shows how much you understand the flow of an organization or workplace and how you will contribute to it. Some questions you can ask:

  ○ What created the need to fill this position? Is it a new position or has someone left the organization?
  ○ Where does this position fit in the overall hierarchy of the organization?
  ○ What are the key skills required to succeed in this job?
  ○ What challenges might I expect to face within the first six months on the job?
  ○ How does this position relate to the achievement of the organization's (or department's, or boss's) goals?
  ○ How would you describe the organization's culture?

You may find yourself interviewing virtually, using technology such as Zoom, rather than appearing in person. This is almost certainly the case during the time of the pandemic, but it may also be your circumstance if you are applying to a job far away from where you live.

To prepare for an online interview, you should follow the same preparation tips as you would for an in-person meeting, but be sure to test the technology ahead of time (including any applications you need to use, passwords you require, microphone, camera, and so on). You can also test to see how your outfit or background appears to the person with whom you will be meeting. There is nothing worse than discovering your interviewer can't hear you properly or that there is anything unprofessional or inappropriate visible to the interviewer.

THE EYES OF PILOTS: A CAREER IN AIR TRAFFIC CONTROL

Simone Brito is from the Netherlands and has worked as an air traffic controller for twenty-three years.

How did you choose air traffic control as a career?

When I was fifteen years old, me and my brother had a chance of our lifetime to visit our American neighbors in the United States. We flew for the first time and I loved it. The world became small and cultures were there to be discovered; it was then when I realized I wanted to work in a multicultural environment. The aviation world was an obvious choice, but as a pilot, being away for longer periods was less appealing. By chance a classmate in my pregrad class showed me the information she had acquired of the air traffic controller student program in Maastricht, the Netherlands. We visited the control center; we had a tour through the building, explanations how the selection, the schooling, and the on-job-training normally would look, and that afternoon we both decided to apply.

Simone Brito is from the Netherlands and has worked as an air traffic controller for twenty-three years. *gorodenkoff/iStock/Getty Images.*

Can you describe your educational background and career path to date?

I finished my preuniversity high school; in the Netherlands it's called "gymnasium." I had a broad package of different subjects including English and mathematics, which were the only subjects required for applying. After my application I was invited for testing, an interview, and a medical test.

What is a typical day on the job for you?

Because planes fly 24/7, I work in shifts. So, my working day could start with an early morning shift at 6:30. . . . We start every half an hour a new shift. The latest shift finishes at 11:00 p.m.; then the night shift starts till 6:30 a.m. I'm a morning person, so I do prefer the early starts. Out of the house before everybody wakes up, on the road before traffic jams, and finished before the day is over. I start with coming in, in time, so I can read the briefing for that day. It's a way of making sure we are up to date with all possible abnormalities; like airports closed, system changes, weather predictions, etc. Then I go to the position I have toured on and take over from my colleague. I plug in my headset, and from that moment I'm in control. I scan the aircraft in my sector, make a plan, and execute that by telling the pilots where to go and what to do. In a working day I have thirty minutes for briefings, then seven and a half hours planned to work, and within these hours I have a two-hour break. Because of the intensity of the kind of work, we are not allowed to be longer than two hours in one go behind a radar. After the seven and a half hours, I plug out and can go home. . . . I love the fact that you finish work when you plug out; I never take work home.

What's the best or most satisfying part of your job?

That we can really help pilots; we are their eyes in the sky. We know the area, the airports; we gather information regarding turbulence, clouds, and pass that information back to the pilots. When a pilot has problems with the aircraft, we can help and make sure that the airspace is free around him. We can help to get [passengers] safely but also efficiently and comfortably to their destination. That's the biggest satisfaction.

What's the most challenging part or stressful part of your job?

Time is a factor in our job; there is no pause button, so there is always a time pressure. This results often in quick scan, thinking, and reacting. Working with minimum mistakes and always thinking in solutions. The stress levels of me but also of all the colleagues around me can rise very quickly, adrenaline all over.

What has been the most surprising thing about your job?

The fun! Air traffic control, guiding more than five thousand aircraft through the busy skies (in non-COVID times), sounds like a very serious business and it sure is, but working with a multicultural team through busy and stressful moments creates a good trust and a lot of fun in calmer moments.

What kinds of qualities do you consider advantageous to doing your job successfully?

Hmm . . . quick logic thinking, thinking in solutions is definitely an important quality; being flexible and being a good team player is also an advantage to have as a quality. Being able to multitask would be good; however, there are studies that state that multitasking doesn't exist. But then being able to switch quickly between tasks is very practical. In the selections they try to find the best matching people. To fit the job but also to fit the teams.

How do you combat burnout?

Getting burned out is a serious risk, especially looking at the stressfulness of this job. My company invests a lot in awareness for the employees—there are mental energy courses, yoga lessons, fitness trainers, and health days. Next to creating time available for staff, my company also invested in goods; we have a gym, sports hall, table tennis in the building that can be used in breaks. So sports is a big counterbalance. Another important factor is sleep. Working in shifts can throw your sleep rhythm overboard, and sleeping areas are available in our building. Myself, I love to spend time in nature with my dog or my horse. I run, I bike, and I do yoga.

How do you see your career evolving in the future?

My career started twenty-three years ago as an air traffic control student; within two years I managed to get my air traffic control license. After some years working on my own license, I became a coach, meaning I was allowed to train trainees on the job. From there I became a training officer, which means I was responsible for all the trainees and coaches in my team. After doing this for some years I moved on to refresher training officer, which means I was preparing the yearly refresher training for all air traffic controllers in my sector and now I'm planned to do my supervisor course, which will start later this year. I'm very excited about this, since it's the first step outside of the training area. So although there are many career possibilities inside this job, I am and I will always stay to be an air traffic controller.

Summary

Congratulations on working through the book! You should now have a strong idea of your career goals within the air transport field, and how to realize them. In this chapter, we covered how to present yourself as the right candidate to a potential employer—and these strategies are also relevant if you are applying to a college or another form of training. Here are some tips to sum it up:

- Your résumé should be concise and focused on only relevant aspects of your work experience or education. Although you can include some personal hobbies or details, they should be related to the job and your qualifications for it.
- Take your time with all your professional documents—your résumé, you cover letter, your LinkedIn profile—and be sure to proofread very carefully to avoid embarrassing and sloppy mistakes.
- Prepare yourself for an interview, anticipating the types of questions you will be asked and coming up with professional and meaningful responses.
- Equally, prepare some questions for you to ask your potential employer at the interview. This will show you have a good understanding and interest in the organization and what role you would have in it.
- Always follow up after an interview with a letter or an email. An email is the fastest way to express your gratitude for the interviewer's time and restate your interest in the position.
- Dress appropriately for an interview and pay extra attention to tidiness and hygiene.
- Be wary of what you share on social media sites while job searching. Most employers research candidates online, and what you have shared will influence their idea of who you are and what it would be like to work with you.

You've chosen to pursue a career in a competitive, challenging, but also broad and exciting field. I wish you great success in your future.

Appendix

Additional Resources

The following websites, magazines, and organizations can help you further investigate and educate yourself on air transportation–related topics, all of which will help you as you take the next steps in your career, now and throughout your professional life.

Organizations

AIR LINE PILOTS ASSOCIATION, INTERNATIONAL (ALPA)

ALPA is the world's largest airline pilot union, representing and advocating for more than sixty-one thousand pilots at thirty-eight US and Canadian airlines. ALPA provides three critical services to its members: airline safety, security, and pilot assistance; representation; and advocacy. https://www.alpa.org/.

INTERNATIONAL AIR TRANSPORT ASSOCIATION (IATA)

The IATA is the trade association for the world's airlines, representing some 290 airlines, or 82 percent of total air traffic. It supports many areas of aviation activity and helps formulate industry policy on critical aviation issues. https://www.iata.org/.

AEROSPACE INDUSTRIES ASSOCIATION (AIA)

The AIA provides a forum for government and industry representatives to exchange views and resolve problems on noncompetitive matters related to the aerospace and defense industry. https://www.aia-aerospace.org/.

NATIONAL AIR TRAFFIC CONTROLLERS ASSOCIATION (NATCA)

The NATCA is a membership-owned organization that advances the status, professionalism, and working conditions of all air traffic controllers and other aviation safety–related employees through collective bargaining and political action. https://www.natca.org/.

ASSOCIATION OF FLIGHT ATTENDANTS CWA (AFA-CWA)

The AFA-CWA is the flight attendant union organized by flight attendants for flight attendants. It represents nearly fifty thousand flight attendants at seventeen airlines. https://www.afacwa.org/.

Publications

WINGS MAGAZINE

A bimonthly Canadian magazine that focuses on stories related to business and commercial aviation. https://www.wingsmagazine.com/.

INTERNATIONAL AIRPORT REVIEW

A leading source of news and information for the airport and aviation community, covering all the latest breaking news in passenger experience, airport business, sustainability, terminal operations, airside operations, and construction and design. https://www.internationalairportreview.com/.

Notes

Introduction

1. International Air Transport Association, "Air Passenger Market Analysis," April 2020, accessed June 18, 2021, https://www.iata.org/en/iata-repository/publications/economic-reports/air-passenger-monthly-analysis---apr-20202/; "Air Passenger Market Analysis," August 2020, accessed June 18, 2021, https://www.iata.org/en/iata-repository/publications/economic-reports/air-passenger-monthly-analysis---august-2020/.

2. Data USA, "Air Transportation," accessed July 5, 2021, https://datausa.io/profile/naics/air-transportation.

3. Statista.com, "Number of Public and Private Airports in the United States from 1990 to 2020," accessed June 18, 2021, https://www.statista.com/statistics/183496/number-of-airports-in-the-united-states-since-1990/.

Chapter 1

1. Scott Mall, "Flashback Friday: The History of Air Freight," FreightWaves, May 24, 2019, accessed August 2, 2021, https://www.freightwaves.com/news/flashback-friday-the-history-of-air-freight.

Chapter 2

1. Jane E. Shersher, "Self Care Tips for Social Workers," SocialWorkLicensure.org, accessed April 21, 2021, https://socialworklicensure.org/articles/self-care-tips/.

Chapter 3

1. Steven R. Antonoff, "College Personality Quiz," *U.S. News & World Report*, July 31, 2018, accessed May 21, 2021, https://www.usnews.com/education/best-col leges/right-school/choices/articles/college-personality-quiz.

2. Alex Gailey, "Taking a Gap Year during Coronavirus? Here's How to Make the Most of It," NextAdvisor, September 29, 2020, accessed May 21, 2021, https://time.com/nextadvisor/in-the-news/gap-year-coronavirus/.

3. Claudia Hammond, "Does Reading Fiction Make Us Better People?," BBC.com, June 3, 2019, accessed March 2, 2021, https://www.bbc.com/future/article/20190523-does-reading-fiction-make-us-better-people.

4. FairTest, "1,425+ Accredited, 4-Year Colleges & Universities with ACT/SAT-Optional Testing Policies for Fall, 2022 Admissions," updated May 17, 2021, accessed May 21, 2021, https://fairtest.org/university/optional.

5. TheBestColleges.org, "The Top 25 Colleges for Aviation Degrees," accessed September 17, 2021, https://www.thebestcolleges.org/rankings/the-top-25-colleges-for-aviation-degrees/.

6. Farran Powell and Emma Kerr, "See the Average College Tuition in 2020–2021," *U.S. News & World Report*, September 14, 2020, accessed May 2, 2021, https://www.usnews.com/education/best-colleges/paying-for-college/articles/paying-for-college-infographic.

7. Powell and Kerr, "Average College Tuition."

8. Emma Kerr, "How Colleges Are Adjusting Their 2021–2022 Tuition," *U.S. News & World Report*, January 21, 2021, accessed May 2, 2021, https://www.usnews.com/education/best-colleges/paying-for-college/articles/how-colleges-are-adjusting-their-2021-2022-tuition.

Chapter 4

1. Alison Doyle, "Student Resume Examples, Templates, and Writing Tips," TheBalanceCareers.com, accessed May 21, 2021, https://www.thebalancecareers.com/student-resume-examples-and-templates-2063555.

2. Indeed.com, "How to Write a Pilot Resume," accessed September 3, 2021, https://www.indeed.com/career-advice/resumes-cover-letters/pilot-resume.

3. LiveCareer.com, "Top 20 Airport Resume Objective Examples You Can Use," accessed September 3, 2021, https://bestresumeobjectiveexamples.com/top-20-airport-resume-objective-examples-you-can-use/.

4. Joshua Waldman, *Job Searching with Social Media for Dummies* (Hoboken, NJ: Wiley, 2013).

5. SecurityMagazine.com, "70 Percent of Employers Check Candidates' Social Media Profiles," September 23, 2018, accessed May 21, 2021, https://www.security magazine.com/gdpr-policy?url=https%3A%2F%2Fwww.securitymagazine.com %2Farticles%2F89441-percent-of-employers-check-candidates-social-media-profiles.

6. Alice A. M. Underwood, "9 Things to Avoid on Social Media while Looking for a New Job," Glassdoor, January 3, 2018, accessed October 30, 2020, https://www .glassdoor.com/blog/things-to-avoid-on-social-media-job-search/.

Glossary

aerospace engineering. A branch of engineering that deals with the design, development, testing, and production of aircraft and related systems.

aircraft and avionics mechanic. A mechanic trained to perform scheduled maintenance, make repairs, and complete inspection of aircraft.

airfield operations specialist. A person whose job it is to ensure that commercial and military aircrafts take off and land safely.

air freight. The goods carried by aircraft.

airline. A company providing a regular public service of air transport on one or more routes.

airline hub. An airport that airlines use outside their headquarters.

airport manager. The decision-makers and policy-makers of airports. They oversee the management of each airport department.

air traffic controller. A person whose job it is to monitor and control air traffic to ensure safe and orderly movement within and between airports.

air transport. The movement of aircraft carrying passengers, cargo, or mail.

bachelor's degree. A four-year degree awarded by a college or university.

bankruptcy. A legal proceeding involving a person or business that is unable to repay their outstanding debts.

burnout. Feeling of physical and emotional exhaustion caused by overworking.

cabin crew. The members of an aircraft crew who attend to passengers. See also *flight attendant.*

campus. The location of a school, college, or university.

career assessment test. A test that asks questions particularly geared to identify skills and interests to help inform the test taker on what type of career would suit them.

cargo. The goods transported by an aircraft.

colleagues. The people with whom you work.

commercial airline. The area of aviation that deals with the transport of passengers or multiple loads of cargo.

community college. A two-year college that awards associate's degrees.

copilot. A first officer in a flight crew that works to assist the captain in safely navigating the plane.

cover letter. A document that usually accompanies a résumé and allows a candidate applying to a job, school, or internship an opportunity to describe their motivation and qualifications.

educational background. The degrees a person has earned and schools attended.

empathy. The quality of being able to understand the feelings of another person.

entry level. A position in a career usually held by a person who is just starting out in their professional life, with their first professional job. Usually this indicates a lower salary and level of responsibility to start than jobs held by more experienced workers.

Federal Aviation Administration (FAA). The agency of the US Department of Transportation responsible for the regulation and oversight of civil aviation within the US, as well as operation and development of the National Airspace System.

financial aid. Various means of receiving financial support for the purposes of attending school. This can be a grant or scholarship, for example.

flight attendant. A member of an aircraft crew who attends to passengers. See also *cabin crew*.

gap year. A year between high school and higher education or employment during which a person can explore their passions and interests, often while traveling.

General Education Development (GED) degree. A degree earned that is the equivalent to a high school diploma without graduating from high school.

industry. The people and activities involved in one type of business, such as the business of air transport.

in-state school. A nonprivate college that exists in the state in which you are a resident. In-state schools offer lower tuitions to state residents.

internship. A work experience opportunity that lasts for a set period of time and can be paid or unpaid.

interpersonal skills. The ability to communicate and interact with other people in an effective manner.

interviewing. A part of the job-seeking process in which a candidate meets with a potential employer, usually face-to-face, to discuss their work experience and education and seek information about the position.

job market. A market in which employers search for employees and employees search for jobs.

major. The subject or course of study in which you choose to earn your degree.

master's degree. A degree that is sought by those who have already earned a bachelor's degree in order to further their education.

mindfulness. The practice of focusing awareness on the present moment while calmly acknowledging and accepting one's feelings, thoughts, and bodily sensations, used as a therapeutic technique.

networking. The processes of building, strengthening, and maintaining professional relationships as a way to further your career goals.

out-of-state school. A nonprivate college that exists in a state other than the one in which you are a resident. These schools have higher tuitions for those who are not residents of that state.

pilot. A person who operates the flying controls of an aircraft.

résumé. A document, usually one page, that outlines a candidate's professional experience and education and that is designed to give potential employers a sense of that person's qualifications.

social media. Websites and applications that enable users to create and share content online for networking and social-sharing purposes. Examples include Facebook, LinkedIn, Twitter, and Instagram.

Transportation Security Administration (TSA). An agency of the US Department of Homeland Security that has authority over the security of the traveling public in the US.

transport security screener. A person who screens passengers, baggage, and cargo to check for compliance with rules and regulations for flight safety regarding objects on the aircraft.

tuition. The money you have to pay for education, be it a university degree or a certification.

work culture. A concept that defines the beliefs, philosophy, thought processes, and attitudes of employees in a particular organization.

Bibliography

Antonoff, Steven R. "College Personality Quiz." *U.S. News & World Report*, July 31, 2018. Accessed May 20, 2021. https://www.usnews.com/educa tion/best-colleges/right-school/choices/articles/college-personality-quiz.

TheBestColleges.org. "The Top 25 Colleges for Aviation Degrees." Accessed September 17, 2021. https://www.thebestcolleges.org/rankings/the-top -25-colleges-for-aviation-degrees/.

Bureau of Labor Statistics. "Aerospace Engineer." Accessed July 5, 2021. https:// www.bls.gov/ooh/architecture-and-engineering/aerospace-engineers.htm.

———. "Airfield Operations Specialists." Accessed July 5, 2021. https://www .bls.gov/oes/current/oes532022.htm.

———. "Flight Attendants." Accessed July 5, 2021. https://www.bls.gov/ooh /transportation-and-material-moving/flight-attendants.htm.

Data USA. "Air Transportation." Accessed July 5, 2021. https://datausa.io/pro file/naics/air-transportation.

Doyle, Alison. "Student Resume Examples, Templates, and Writing Tips." The BalanceCareers.com. Accessed May 21, 2021. https://www.thebalance careers.com/student-resume-examples-and-templates-2063555.

FairTest. "1,425+ Accredited, 4-Year Colleges & Universities with ACT/ SAT-Optional Testing Policies for Fall, 2022 Admissions." Updated May 17, 2021. Accessed May 21, 2021. https://fairtest.org/university/optional.

Gailey, Alex. "Taking a Gap Year during Coronavirus? Here's How to Make the Most of It." NextAdvisor. September 29, 2020. Accessed May 21, 2021. https://time.com/nextadvisor/in-the-news/gap-year-coronavirus/.

Hammond, Claudia. "Does Reading Fiction Make Us Better People?" BBC. com. June 3, 2019. Accessed March 2, 2021. https://www.bbc.com /future/article/20190523-does-reading-fiction-make-us-better-people.

Indeed.com. "How to Write a Pilot Resume." Accessed September 3, 2021. https://www.indeed.com/career-advice/resumes-cover-letters/pilot-resume.

International Air Transport Association. "Air Passenger Market Analysis."
    April 2020. Accessed June 18, 2021. https://www.iata.org/en/iata-repos
    itory/publications/economic-reports/air-passenger-monthly-analysis
    ---apr-20202/.

————. "Air Passenger Market Analysis." August 2020. Accessed June 18,
    2021. https://www.iata.org/en/iata-repository/publications/economic
    -reports/air-passenger-monthly-analysis---august-2020/.

Kerr, Emma. "How Colleges Are Adjusting Their 2021–2022 Tuition." *U.S.
    News & World Report*, January 21, 2021. Accessed May 2, 2021. https://
    www.usnews.com/education/best-colleges/paying-for-college/articles
    /how-colleges-are-adjusting-their-2021-2022-tuition.

LiveCareer.com. "Top 20 Airport Resume Objective Examples You Can Use."
    Accessed September 3, 2021. https://bestresumeobjectiveexamples.com
    /top-20-airport-resume-objective-examples-you-can-use/.

Mall, Scott. "Flashback Friday: The History of Air Freight." FreightWaves. May
    24, 2019. Accessed August 2, 2021. https://www.freightwaves.com/news
    /flashback-friday-the-history-of-air-freight.

Powell, Farran, and Emma Kerr. "See the Average College Tuition in 2020–
    2021." *U.S. News & World Report*, September 14, 2020. Accessed May
    2, 2021. https://www.usnews.com/education/best-colleges/paying-for-col
    lege/articles/paying-for-college-infographic.

SecurityMagazine.com. "70 Percent of Employers Check Candidates' Social
    Media Profiles." September 23, 2018. Accessed May 21, 2021. https://
    www.securitymagazine.com/gdpr-policy?url=https%3A%2F%2Fwww
    .securitymagazine.com%2Farticles%2F89441-percent-of-employers
    -check-candidates-social-media-profiles.

Shersher, Jane E. "Self Care Tips for Social Workers." SocialWorkLicensure
    .org. Accessed April 21, 2021. https://socialworklicensure.org/articles/self
    -care-tips/.

Statista.com. "Number of Public and Private Airports in the United States from
    1990 to 2020." Accessed June 18, 2021. https://www.statista.com/statistics
    /183496/number-of-airports-in-the-united-states-since-1990/.

Underwood, Alice A. M. "9 Things to Avoid on Social Media while Looking for a
    New Job." Glassdoor. January 3, 2018. Accessed October 30, 2020. https://
    www.glassdoor.com/blog/things-to-avoid-on-social-media-job-search/.

Waldman, Joshua. *Job Searching with Social Media for Dummies*. Hoboken, NJ:
    Wiley, 2013.

About the Author

Tracy Brown Hamilton is a writer, editor, and journalist based in the Netherlands. She has written several books on topics ranging from careers to media, economics to pop culture. She lives with her husband and three children.

www.ingramcontent.com/pod-product-compliance
Ingram Content Group UK Ltd.
Pitfield, Milton Keynes, MK11 3LW, UK
UKHW041430090725
460600UK00020B/156